Keep the Spirit!

A Guide to Practicing What You Preached for Returned Missionaries

Ralph G. Degn

Keep the Spirit!

A Guide to Practicing What You Preached for Returned Missionaries

Ralph G. Degn

First Printing: March 1997

International Standard Book Number:
0-88290-598-8

Horizon Publishers' Catalog and Order Number:
1077

Printed and distributed
in the United States of America by

& Distributors, Incorporated

Mailing Address:
P.O. Box 490
Bountiful, Utah 84011-0490

Street Address:
50 South 500 West
Bountiful, Utah 84010

Local Phone: (801) 295-9451
Toll Free: 1 (866) 818-6277
FAX: (801) 295-0196

E-mail: horizonp@burgoyne.com
Internet: http://www.horizonpublishers.biz

Contents

ABOUT THE COVER

Christopher Degn, the author's son, is welcomed home from his mission to France by his mother.

1

INTRODUCTION

Men and women who turn their lives over to God find He can make a lot more out of their lives than they can.
—President Ezra Taft Benson

When I was called as a new mission president, I wanted to pass along in my final interview with our departing missionaries some tried and proven keys to achieving success in the "real world" once those young warriors were released back into it.

At the time of my call, I had served about eight years in bishoprics in university singles wards, and I was currently bishop of a ward that was composed of about 95% returned missionaries. Since I was seeing many of these recently returned missionaries (RMs) enjoying excellence in the various areas of their lives—studies, employment, social life—I decided to ask them what were the factors that were bringing them this success. The list these great RMs gave me are the topics of chapters three through sixteen.

The last seven chapters, ten through sixteen, are longer than the previous ones. This is because I've found that many RMs sometimes neglected these areas, although a knowledge of these subjects is essential for living successfully in the "real world."

I put the topics of chapters three through sixteen together, printed them up in a little booklet and took it into the mission field, handing one out to each missionary in my final interview. Since being released as mission president I've expanded the booklet, included experiences from some of our great RMs of the Brazil Sao Paulo North Mission, suggestions from our four RM sons and RM daughter, and some of my observations as mission president.

The RMs said that all of these ideas that brought them success in the "real world" could be summarized into one factor—the same factor that brought them success in the mission field—**KEEP THE SPIRIT!** It doesn't matter whether you're in the mission field or in the "real world," keeping the Spirit is essential for excellence. These ideas are the ones that the RMs told me worked the best for keeping themselves happy, properly oriented, and "in tune" once they returned to the challenges of everyday living.

Like many other LDS Church leaders, I have heard sad laments such as the following many hundreds of times:

> "Bishop, I just don't have the Spirit any more."
>
> "I've lost the Spirit I had on my mission and I can't get it back. Can you help me, Bishop?"
>
> "How can I feel like I'm doing something important again?"
>
> "How can I be sure if this is the person I'm to marry?"
>
> "It all seems so cut-throat in school; how do I compete and still keep the Spirit?"
>
> "I can't believe the lying out there. How do I get the business and still stay honest?"

The solutions to the above problems in the "real world" are the same ones that brought you success in the mission field. And they all boil down to the same answer: **KEEP THE SPIRIT!** You therefore have to stay disciplined enough to do two things:

1. Do the things that qualify you for the Spirit.
2. Keep from doing the things that drive the Spirit away.

Simple? *Yes!* Easy? *No!*

All the RMs I've talked to have agreed that when you return you must be "in the world but not of the world." They typically gave two cautions. (1) It is very easy for you to revert back to your old habits, your "old you," and (2) you cannot "adapt" to the "real world" when you return or you will be committing spiritual suicide. The dictionary defines "adapt" as "adjust, accommodate, conform." Yes, you need to "adjust;" but you must never "accommodate" or "conform" to the "real world."

Because you are an RM, you must stand as a witness of God "at all times and in all things, and in all places that ye may be in" (Mosiah 18:9). And the Lord says you "shall continue in bearing my name before the world, and also to the church. And [you] shall not suppose that [you] can say enough in my cause" (D&C 24:10). If you do otherwise, you cannot keep the Spirit, and will thus lose your ability to achieve excellence.

Up until now, your mission probably was the greatest spiritual experience of your life. But at your homecoming, I hope you won't merely say, "It was the best two years of my life!" I hope you'll also add, "until now." The rest of your life can be even more satisfying if you look at its various activities and seasons the same way you looked at your mission when you had the most satisfying times. You succeeded best—even excelled—when you had the perspective that what you did was a stewardship for the glory of God.

Your life, too, is a stewardship from God. You're here on earth to serve God's purposes. Earth life is not a stage on which to act out your own selfish desires and ambitions. If you look upon all aspects of your life—dating, marriage, education, profession, family life, etc.—as a stewardship or a mission from God, you can develop the correct attitudes to not only succeed, but excel. When you turn any aspect of your life to become self-serving, it becomes spiritually unsatisfying.

Remember, there's a big difference between "self-service" and "selfless service." If you look upon each role in your life as a mission for the glory of God, you will have even greater spiritual rewards and experiences than you did in the mission field. As Steven Covey says, "You won't need to live on the sweet memories and resurrected testimony of your mission days as the source of your spiritual life."[1] You'll be creating "the best two years of your life" as you live each two years.

This book is not a complete list of things to do, or to avoid doing, to keep the Spirit in the "real world." It is a listing of ideas that RMs have shared with me—ideas that have brought them excellence in school, employment, finding "the one," and in other areas of the "real" but sometimes "lone and dreary world." Other ideas could be added. For example, little is said about prayer, even though it is vital in keeping the Spirit. But since almost all of the RMs knew what they had to do to experience successful prayer, not much is said about it.

The order of the chapters is the same priority order given by the returned missionaries who responded to my questions and surveys. My original survey had the "Three Li'l Pigs" first. I was, frankly, surprised that the RMs mentioned these "little indiscretions" first, but upon reflection, I saw the wisdom and honesty in this. I believe the RMs listed them first because of their altered perspective after being home for several months.

My experience as mission president also indicated something about fear needed to be mentioned first, so I added chapter two, "The Big Bad Wolf."

These suggestions have worked for lots of RMs; they are tried and true. And they can be utilized by any Latter-day Saint; they are applicable to everyone who desires to be in tune with the divine promptings they're entitled to receive as confirmed members of the Church. You can use them too, not only as your spiritual survival guide, but to help you succeed and excel in any field of endeavor in the "real world." They truly will help you to

KEEP THE SPIRIT!

2

Defeat Self-Doubt — The Big Bad Wolf —

Who's afraid of the big bad wolf?

If ye are prepared, ye shall not fear.
—Doctrine and Covenants 38:30

The only thing to fear is fear itself.
—Franklin Delano Roosevelt

The "big bad wolf" is a symbol of all the fears Satan will try to get you to feel when, or even before, you return home. The "big bad wolf" will attempt to "blow your house down" before you return to it, and of course, while you're in it. With his blasts of hot air, (or to be more scriptural, with his "shafts in the whirlwind"—Hel. 5:12), Satan will try to get you to be afraid and to doubt. He will "huff n' puff" (or again, to be slightly more scriptural, he "whispereth"—2 Ne. 28:22) in your ear, to get you to think that you lived in a spiritual "house of bricks" in the mission field, but that when you return home you'll only be able to live in a "house of straw." Once you understand this and prepare yourself, you'll know his lies and half-truths are merely a "tempest in a teapot."

He'll try to convince you your spiritual house is made of straw through myths and half-truths he has fabricated, such as the following:

1. *"You're unworthy because you feel the Spirit less now that you're home"* (a half-truth).

Fact: After you return home, you may feel the influence of the Spirit less, but not because you are unworthy. You may feel it less for reasons such as these:

You'll gradually feel the spirit of peace fade that you felt in the final days of your mission. The Lord sent this peace to you to say, "Well done my good and faithful servant, I accept your mission." But once that message has been given, this fading is natural. It shouldn't be construed as your turning unworthy, as Satan will whisper.

As you're released, the mantle of your calling is removed and you'll feel it's absence. Again, Satan will whisper, "If you were really worthy, you wouldn't feel its lack," but he's lying to you.

As you enter back into the "real world" from serving the Lord full-time, you may receive or recognize fewer opportunities to serve, at first. Church service outside of the mission field is usually on a part-time basis. Less service means feeling the Spirit less; it doesn't mean that you are unworthy.

2. Satan will whisper, *"In the mission field, you were 'making a difference,' you were 'affecting people's lives,' you were doing something of 'eternal value.' But now what are you doing? Ha! Merely going to school or working—nothing of real importance."* As a bishop, I've had many RMs tell me they worried about this half-truth.

Fact: What you're doing at home is one of the most important things that all of us come to earth to experience—learning how to "wait upon the Lord." You couldn't do this as well in the mission field because your time and efforts were too concentrated. Yes, things moved quicker in the mission field, and results were more spectacular. But what you're doing in the "lone and dreary world" is of equal value, just different. Those who learn to wait upon the Lord learn one of the stellar qualities in the constellation of charity's attributes—patience! Remember, there are "great things" which the Lord has prepared "for him that waiteth" (D&C 133:45). As you "wait upon the Lord," you learn something that even Adam needed to learn (Moses 5:6), but that Satan never did.

3. A lie: *"You'll fall once you leave the protection of the mission field and get into your 'straw house' in the 'real world,' just as you've seen other RMs fall."*

Fact: You'll live in a spiritual "house of *bricks*" in the "real world" just as much as you did in the mission field, if you do the things to **KEEP THE SPIRIT**!

Yes, it is natural to fear returning home and what you'll find there. I was fearful too when released. It's natural to feel concerned, since it's a new experience. Most people are fearful of new experiences, even people as strong and faithful as the pioneers. A BYU speaker observed:

According to Parley P. Pratt, the pioneers who endured the first terrible winter in the Salt Lake Valley suffered more from fear than from actual hunger. Remember how hungry the Saints were: "The people tried eating crows, thistle tops, bark, roots, and Sego Lily bulbs, anything that might offer nutriment or fill the empty stomach." Yet they suffered most from fear. For "the valley was new," says Bro. Pratt, "ne[i]ther was it proven that grain could be raised."[1]

But your returning home is really just another transfer, this time to an area you'll really love, and to people who love you (although they'll speak a strange language at first).

You have "nothing to fear but fear itself." Remember, the Lord said, "Wherefore be of good cheer, and do not fear, for I the Lord am with you, and will stand by you." (D&C 68:6). And he also instructed the Saints that "If ye are prepared, ye shall not fear" (D&C 38:30). You need not fear because you are well prepared for the "real world" because of your mission experiences.

"Who's afraid of the big bad wolf?" Not you, "not by the hair of your chinney-chin-chin," because you won't be living in a "house of *straw*." You'll be living in a spiritual "house of *bricks*." You'll not only stay prepared, but you'll excel in the "real world," as you do the things that will help you

KEEP THE SPIRIT!

3

CONQUER SELF-INDULGENCE — THE THREE LI'L PIGS —

Cease to be idle; cease to be unclean; cease to find fault one with another; cease to sleep longer than is needful; retire to thy bed early, that ye may not be weary; arise early that your bodies and your minds may be invigorated.

—Doctrine and Covenants 88:124

Along with the "Big Bad Wolf" of fear, the top three things that RMs said contributed first to their spiritual decline once they got home, are what I call "The Three Li'l Pigs." They are not, significantly, any of the "biggies" such as slacking off from praying or from reading the scriptures. It seems everyone knows we need to do these key things so they are kept up, at first.

"The Three Li'l Pigs" are "little," seeming unimportant, self-indulgent "indiscretions," thus their name. But they immediately bring the wolf to your door, and by deception, he blows away your spirituality.

My survey among the RMs showed the very same thing that the Lord had already cautioned the Prophet Joseph Smith against over 150 years ago. "The Three Li'l Pigs" are, by no coincidence, the three admonitions listed above in D&C 88:124—*slothfulness* ("cease to be idle"), *lasciviousness* ("cease to be unclean"), and *sarcasm* ("cease to find fault one with another").

Slothfulness—This is the number one problem—sleeping-in! The many RMs I've interviewed have said that this was the first thing that started them down the road of losing the Spirit. Slothfulness is insidious, creeping up without your being aware of the problem. It seems we all understand that we must pray and search the scriptures, but we somehow don't see the connection between a regular cycle of staying up late and then sleeping-in, and the resulting loss of the Spirit. It's not surprising that the Lord commands us not to do this.

Sleeping-in is made even worse if we allow dark thoughts to roam unbridled in our minds as we lie there before we get up. (See "*Control Your Thoughts*," Chapter Four.)

Lasciviousness—In the parlance of our day, lasciviousness would probably be called "raunchiness" or "smut." Because it is so common now in the media and in entertainment, you definitely need to take steps to keep from being exposed to its debilitating effects on your spirit.

A recent headline had this to say about the MTV Video Music Awards: "Rock 'n' Raunch Highlight MTV Awards." Again, all those I've interviewed have said the raunch in speech and pictures on videos, MTV, music, and movies has "hardened" them to the Spirit. (This is the word they most often used.) As a result, they were unkind, impatient, cynical, sarcastic, and did a host of other selfish acts. They singled out MTV for special mention since raunch appears so often and unexpectedly (as well as at known times), licentiousness masquerading as liberty. As Michael Medved, co-host of the weekly PBS TV SNEAK PREVIEWS, says: "Nothing could stand at a further remove from selflessness and discipline . . . than the masturbatory fantasies that saturate MTV 24 hours a day."[1] The best way to keep raunch out is by the way you keep your own room. (More on this under "*Control Your Thoughts*.")

Some RMs started their fall into raunch by sticking around to watch a video their roommate, also an RM, had rented. "I just returned from my mission and I didn't know what was what yet," they'd tell me. "I thought it would be a good video. After all, he was an RM too and he'd been home a year. And once it started I didn't want to appear 'holier than thou' and leave. I should have, though; now I've got those images in my mind that I have to fight against. They remind and entice me to do wrong things. Sometimes I yield and do them. I wish I'd not seen them."

Sarcasm—Sarcasm, especially in "humor" and especially directed at friends, always is inappropriate, and we're commanded not to use it. The Lord says to "cease to find fault one with another" (D&C 88:124).

Without knowing it, we become accustomed to this seemingly harmless habit and start using sarcasm and cynicism ourselves. You may be immune to sarcasm, but the Spirit isn't. If you use sarcasm, even in jest, or if there is sarcasm present, the Spirit leaves. This is why sitcoms, soaps, and other forms of "entertainment" that use put-downs and other demeaning "comedy" should be avoided. Remember, the Lord's instruction is to "Strengthen your brethren in all your conversation" (D&C 108:7).

Another form of weakening conversation is the use of swearing, vulgar words, crude expressions, and inappropriate jokes we all know to be out of line. It was the prevalence of crude expressions, even from some RMs, that struck me the hardest when I returned home. These terms don't typically appear in a RM's conversation at first, but they can appear later, especially if you've had a problem with this before your mission. Here's what President Hinckley said about this:

> In our dialogues with others we must be an example of the believers . . . I do not hesitate to say that it is wrong, seriously wrong, for any man ordained to the priesthood of God to be guilty of [foul language].[2]

Brigham Young gave a wonderful promise about controlling your speech. Said he, "If you first gain power to check your words, you will then begin to have power to check your judgment."[3] By taming your tongue and refraining from inappropriate comments, you are more receptive to increased inspiration, and therefore you can exercise better judgment. Considering the number of judgments and decisions you make each day, and especially when the two most important judgments you'll ever make in your life (who you marry and what you pursue as a career) will be made soon, wouldn't it be great to make the best ones? You can, by checking your words!

Speaking of whom you're going to marry, if you wonder about the propriety of your speech or your thoughts, remember: "Birds of a feather flock together." As one RM told me, "Will I find a better spouse by saying or thinking this, or will I find a slacker?" You'll only find a spouse as good as you are.

Because Satan has been very successful in getting lots of RMs to fall for "The Three Li'l Pigs," he'll attempt to get you to be a sucker and fall for them too. However, since "forewarned is forearmed," you can stay strong and

KEEP THE SPIRIT!

4

Control Your Thoughts — Beyond the Barricades —

Will you join in our crusade? Who will be strong and stand with me?
Beyond the barricades is there a world you long to see?
Then join in the fight that will give you the right to be free!
—*Les Miserables*

. . . if ye do not watch yourselves, and your thoughts, . . . ye must perish."
—*Mosiah 4:30*

At one of our ward leadership conferences, we used the above quote from the powerful song, "Do You Hear the People Sing" from "Les Mis" as our theme. As our leaders answered then, you need to answer now. What are the thoughts "that will give you the right to be free," so you can be part of the "world you long to see"? What thoughts will help or hinder you "to be free"?

All this has to do with the word "barricades" in the above quote from "Les Mis." (By the way, President Kimball voiced his personal opinion of the great Gospel message in the book *Les Miserables.*[1]) Barricades can either help or hinder us. In this chapter, we're going to talk about helpful barricades; in the following chapter, we'll discuss the harmful kind.

What is a helpful barricade? It is a protective wall that encloses you, keeping you safe from danger outside. Although the situation is apparently contradictory, "to be free" you need a strong, protective barricade around you.

Inside, you're "free to act." But outside, instead of being free, you can't always control the situation; you're being "acted upon." If you let your barricade down and let danger inside, then you're no longer free nor safe. You must constantly maintain the barricade strong in order to keep you safe inside.

A ship illustrates the importance of a barricade. You will literally sink and swim (or drown) if you let water past the wall of your boat which is barricading you from the sea.

All the water in the sea
Can never sink the smallest ship.
'Tis only when it comes inside,
You'll be in water past your lip.

The barricade you're to build around you is thought control. It will shield you from the "fiery darts of the adversary" (1 Ne. 15:24). With this barricade, you'll be free to act for yourself and not be acted upon (2 Ne. 2:26). Losing their thought control is typically the first thing RMs do which causes them to lose the Spirit and yield to the "Big Bad Wolf." But the first symptoms of this loss that show up are fear and the other things mentioned in "The Three Li'l Pigs." That's why they are mentioned first.

I'd like to tell you about a young man who spent a lot of time enclosed in another kind of barricade—a state prison. He told me some interesting things about the barricade of thought control. He said even though he had been "kind of" in control of his thoughts, he did not follow the warnings of loving parents and church leaders to always stay within the safety of this barricade. Instead, he wanted to think about things outside the barricade. Soon these thoughts became so compelling he wanted to do them. "I wanted to have the rush of getting away with it," he said. The rush became addictive. He said, "You need to not only think about the things you should, but also don't think about the things you shouldn't." He only did the first part, "kind of."

Without a strong thought-control barricade, you are just as vulnerable to defeat as ancient cities were without a strong wall. As the proverb says, "He that hath no rule over his own spirit is like a city that is broken down, and without walls" (Prov. 25:28).

Matt Bahr, the great place kicker for the New York Giants, knew the necessity of controlling thoughts, especially when the pressure was on. Thought control made it possible for him to be "free to act" and not be "acted upon." In the 1991 Super Bowl playoffs, he scored all 15 points for the Giants as they won the NFC championship. Here's a newspaper account of what happened.

> New York Giants kicker Matt Bahr was talking to himself as he stood alone on the torn turf. And why not? Nobody else would. The players of his field-goal unit, his best friends, looked away; his teammates on the sidelines knelt in prayer. The opposing team members were either beckoning to the crowd or screaming obscenities at him. "You're aware of the situation," Bahr said later, "But you try not to let it change anything."[2]

What?! "Not let it change anything?!" Not let the tens of thousands of rabid fans who are shouting at you, not let the obscenities by opposing team members shouted at you, not let the thousands of dollars that will be won or lost on this kick, affect you?! Not let the pressure of the situation "not change anything!" You've got to be kidding!

How does anyone develop that much self-control? By having built a barricade of thought control around yourself so you can be "free to act" and not be "acted upon," no matter what may be happening around you.

There are two things that greatly facilitate controlling your thoughts: (1) what you listen to, and (2) what you look at. It's much easier to control your thoughts if you first control these.

What You Listen To—Music is the main thing here. Since music appeals mainly to the emotions, and the emotions are what empower your actions, whatever you listen to exerts a powerful force not only on your thoughts, but on your actions too. Since I've been in the entertainment business all my life, I'm very familiar with the effects of music on people.

As an RM I played dinner music at Grand Canyon Lodge. There were two main times when people were being seated, and I'd play upbeat music during this time to get them to sit down faster. Once their orders were taken, I'd play some laid-back music so they wouldn't become impatient and anxious about receiving their dinner. Once their dinners were served, I'd play upbeat music again so they would eat faster. If I varied this routine, people would slow down or speed up at the wrong times! I'd then have the waitresses, chefs, and the manager mad at me because of the lost tips and fewer customers!

For many years I've improvised piano music for melodrama productions. Depending on the music played, the same acting will produce either laughs of tears. And lack of music, or inappropriate music, can literally break a scene. It has been a heady experience to realize that I could manipulate the emotions of 250 people without them knowing it. Even more amazing was the fact that most weren't even aware that they were hearing any music at all!

As CEO of a fireworks manufacturing company for many years, I was responsible for entertaining millions of people with our fireworks shows. Since fireworks use the four elements of drama—light, sound, movement, and timing—we had to follow these same principles in order to succeed. When we combined our shows with music, we needed to also follow correct musical principles for success. Again, the dramatic moment, even with something as spectacular as fireworks, could be broken if inappropriate music was played.

My point in all this is: whether you are male or female, old or young, and whether you like or dislike music, even if you're unaware you're hearing it, music has a powerful effect on you. I've seen it first-hand for many years.

All music has, more or less, either a good or bad effect on us—but it's not neutral. Even the ancient Greeks understood this because they prohibited certain elements of the three main physical aspects of music (melody, harmony, rhythm) because of their adverse effect.

Besides these three physical elements of music, there is also a fourth element: the spiritual. All things have both a spiritual and then a physical creation (Moses 3:5). The spiritual creation is the part that gives life to anything, like our body, and music is no exception. It is this part that is the most powerful influence on us, either for good or for evil. It is the spiritual part that carries the intentions of the composer and the performer to the listener. The Greeks also understood the power of this spiritual aspect because they prohibited any person to teach or perform music that was not "a good person of high integrity and good intentions," as Aristotle explained in his classic treatise on music.

Moroni says the method by which you can judge anything is by what it "inviteth" or "persuadeth" you to *do* (Moroni 7:12-19). Thus, if music is good, as Michael Ballam says, you'll feel the love of God. If music is bad, you'll feel the hate of Satan. When we feel the love of God in music we are really hearing the voice of God. And when we feel the hate of Satan in music, we are really hearing the voice of Satan. Even the animals recognize the difference, as shown in the following story told by Brother Ballam.

> In 1985, about 3,000 Beluga whales were trapped under the ice in the Bering Straits. Scientists were concerned because these whales are an endangered species. The USA, Russia, England, and Scandinavian countries sent ice-breakers to make a trail through the ice. Because whales guide by sound, with all of the noise made by the ships, the whales became confused and didn't know where to go. The whales began to be agitated. Some began to suffocate since they couldn't rise to the surface to breathe because the ice was re-freezing. Since whales communicate by sounds and singing, the scientists decided to play music underneath the water to guide the whales to the trail. First, folk music was played, but the whales only became more agitated. Then Jazz was played because of the strong rhythms, to no avail. Rock was played, but the whales turned aggressive. Finally one well-informed scientist played some Beethoven symphonies. The whales followed the sound and swam to liberty. The animals recognized the voice of God and followed it.[3]

Today there is lots of good music around, in many different styles, that can inspire us. But there is also lots around that has the opposite effect. As music, it is well crafted—some of it is even ingenious. No one could write better, even Mozart. Would Satan use anything less than the best? But it is spiritual suicide if you listen to it because of its great power from Satan. John Lennon, Mick Jagger, and various heavy metal groups have even acknowledged that the influence for much of their music comes from the "dark side."[4]

Satan hates young people, especially RMs, because he knows that it is you, not us old folks, who can stop him. Elder LeGrand Richards said that "When Satan and his followers were cast out, they brought with them the knowledge that they had in the pre-mortal life and they knew whom they had fought against.[5] Thus, Satan knows who are the best soldiers in the struggle between good and evil. So, if you were Satan's commander-in-chief, which soldiers would you want to kill? Right! And Satan is trying to spiritually kill RMs through the power of the dark side of music. Satan knows you, how courageous you were and are, and what and who you can become. Do you?

Listen to uplifting music, shun the raunchy stuff. Go through your collection and do some weeding if necessary. There are only two kinds of music: that which edifies and that which tears down. There is no such thing as neutral music. Aristotle, Moroni, Bach, and the Lord understood this, and so should you.

What You See—In Orson Hyde's account of the First Vision, he makes this interesting observation: "The adversary benighted his mind with doubts, and brought to his soul all kinds of improper pictures."[6] This has always been one of Satan's most successful ways—even with the prophets—to thwart our keeping the Spirit.

What you see in your room greatly affects your thoughts. Before you put anything in your room ask yourself these questions: Does it inspire you, help you to think righteous thoughts, and keep the Spirit? Or does it promote covetous, selfish, or carnal thoughts?

I've had some interesting experiences as bishop when I've visited some apartments. One roommate would immobilize me up front (or outside) and with much loud talking, try to drown out the ripping sounds I'd hear coming from the back halls and rooms before I was allowed inside.

I hope you will take President Kimball's advice and have a picture of a temple on the wall.[7] A picture of the Savior, along with some other inspiring posters, would definitely uplift you too.

Keeping your place neat, clean, and organized helps promote the feeling that you can overcome the problems that seem to disorganize your life. A clean room also helps keep you from taking short-cuts in your studies or work. I learned this from an old-timer in my profession when I first started out. He said, "You can tell a lot about a guy's product by looking at his shop. If he takes short-cuts by not taking the time to keep it clean, you can be sure he's taking short-cuts in his product too. Don't buy anything from someone who keeps a dirty shop."

Combining sight and sound, videos, TV, and movies can help you keep your thoughts clean or dirty. Be extremely selective in what you choose. The Book of Mormon repeatedly warns Church members that because they have "so great light and knowledge," they're not to "give way" to lasciviousness and indolence (Al. 45:12; 47:36). We've talked about these twin temptations before in "The Three Li'l Pigs," Chapter 3.

As one RM told me, "Your room will either be a temple or a den of thieves, depending on what you allow there." He then went on to paraphrase President McKay by saying, "What you really are is what you listen to or look at—and thus think about—when you're alone in your room."

Remember, just as your physical body is influenced by and ultimately composed of what you eat and drink, so your spiritual body is influenced by and ultimately composed of what you hear, see, and think.

Ask yourself the question Mormon asks in 8:38: Are you ashamed to take upon you the name of Christ? Make your room a spiritual barricade against sights and sounds (including language) that incline you to "give way" to raunch.

You may feel you're not affected by bad language or other raunch because it's so common. You may be immune, but the Spirit isn't, and he won't stay around where he feels uncomfortable. Yes, there are times when you cannot help but hear or see raunch, but most times you can control it. When you "give way" to raunch, the Spirit leaves and you are left on your own.

Thoughts follow the law of the harvest. This means that you'll not only reap the same kind of thoughts you typically think, but reap them in abundance. A seed doesn't merely return one seed, but many. When you plant one bean, you don't reap one bean; you reap a bean stalk full of hundreds of beans, each a potential seed.

Here's a suggestion from Dr. Alan McGinnis that really helps in controlling thoughts. Put a rubber band on your wrist and wear it 24 hours a day. When you catch yourself in an inappropriate thought, snap the rubber band and replace the negative thought with a positive one. After a few weeks of this, you'll be very aware of your thinking.[8] Soon you'll be able to monitor and replace without the rubber band and build a strong barricade of thought control.

To show that you choose and control the thoughts you think, here's a story from Bishop Clarke about the on-court activity of two professional tennis players—Bjorn Borg and John McEnroe.

> You probably remember Borg as the Swede who rarely showed any emotion on the tennis court and who decided never to be angry at the linesmen and the umpire. But Borg's self-control was made, not born. Borg displayed an on-court temper similar to McEnroe's when he was in his early teens in Sweden when he was known for his swearing and throwing rackets. At the age of 13 he was suspended by his tennis club for six months. And his parents supported that expulsion by locking up his racket and refusing to let him play at all.

Borg now says that he learned his lesson and simply decided from that day forward to control his temper—and he did. By contrast, John McEnroe indicated in a recent "60 Minutes" interview that he believes he is "addicted" to his outbursts of temper.

It is, however, interesting to note that McEnroe said the one time he did control his temper was when he played Borg because "he couldn't afford to waste one bit of energy when playing Borg."[9]

The diagram on this page illustrates the preeminent place your thoughts occupy in your life. Your conscious mind governs the actions, thoughts, and feelings of the outer triangle. The subconscious mind governs the skills, attitudes and disposition of the inner triangle. Ultimately, all your conscious and unconscious activities—habits, attitudes, skills, disposition, actions, feelings—everything that goes on inside you, is governed by your thoughts!

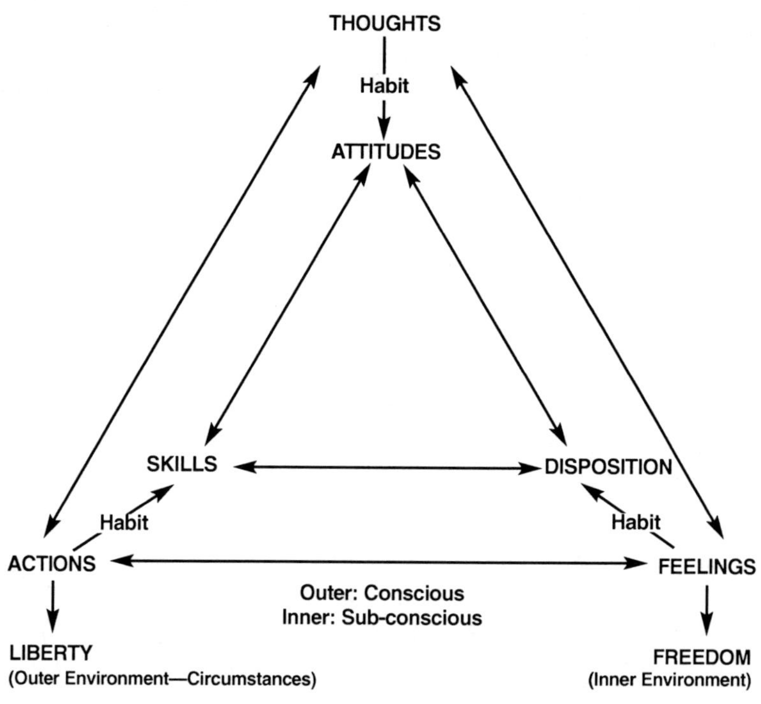

***Attitude**—A habit of thoughts.* The dictionary defines attitude as: "(1) A state of mind with regard to some matter that is deliberately chosen. (2) Aviation: the orientation of an aircraft's wings relative to the horizon." Whether guiding a plane or a life, the pilot who doesn't control the attitude of his craft is headed for a crash. Your attitude literally determines the altitude of your plane or your life. Deciding beforehand what your attitude will be gives you the peace of mind to do your best.

***Skill**—A habit of actions.*

***Disposition**—A habit of feeling.* Ultimately you choose to be either characteristically sweet, sour, etc. Your general facial expression—your countenance—is governed by how frequently you feel certain feelings and think certain thoughts.

You must learn to control your thoughts and to "act . . . and not to be acted upon" (2 Ne. 2:26). If you don't control your thoughts, you will have a mental environment where the Spirit feels uncomfortable, and he will leave. You'll thus be left alone to suffer the buffetings of Satan, and to struggle with your own strength and "wisdom," or lack thereof.

"Watch yourself" by maintaining a strong barricade of thought control so you can

KEEP THE SPIRIT!

5

REPENT CONTINUALLY — COME UNTO CHRIST FIRST —

O all ye that are spared because ye were more righteous than they, will ye not now return unto me, and repent of your sins, and be converted, that I may heal you?

—3 Nephi 9:13

Yea, come unto Christ, and be perfected in him and deny yourselves of all ungodliness . . .

—Moroni 10:32

If you slip and go beyond the helpful barricade of spiritual security discussed in the last chapter, you need to be honest with yourself and with the Lord, and you need to come unto Him and repent. If you fail to do so, you really will be constructing a harmful barricade around yourself.

Harmful barricades are made up of things of your own doing that keep you from "fulfilling the measure of your creation." They are composed of your sins, your transgressions, your indiscretions, your bad judgments, and your follies. If you don't repent of them, you'll be held a prisoner, and you'll be your own jailer. But repentance is the key "that will give you the right to be free," as you go "beyond" your self-imposed harmful barricades.

Repentance! How many times did you preach this essential principle in the mission field? So how can you, one who is so familiar with this principle, need repentance? This was the main hang-up that RMs said kept them from repenting: "Who me? I don't need to repent, at least not until I do something really serious." Learn and remember this basic gospel principle: all of us, including you, are in need of repentance all the time. Let me paraphrase a familiar scripture for you:

And the RMs will he pacify, and lull them away into carnal security, that they will say:

All is well with me; yea, I prosper, all is well—and thus the devil cheateth their souls, and leadeth them away carefully down to hell . . . and thus he whispereth in their ears, until he grasps them with his awful chains, from which there is no deliverance. (2 Ne. 28:21-22, *mais ou menos*).

The next most serious hang-up that RMs had about repenting was that they felt their bishop would think less of them—not necessarily think that they were a "bad" person, but that they were someone that was weak or could not be trusted. Along with this line of rationalization was the thought that they first needed to "get it under control," then they would see the bishop, thus having some credibility as a person who made a mistake but who was trying. Whoa! This is really "stinkin' thinkin'!" This is what the Lord warned about in D&C 121:37 when He cautioned us not to "undertake to cover our sins, or to gratify our pride, our vain ambition." Here are some other "stinkin' thinkin'" comments I've heard:

"Bishop, I know I should have come to you sooner, but I was afraid you would release me."

"I thought you'd think less of me; after all, I am an RM."

"I was just too embarrassed to talk about those things."

You cannot repent until you first "come unto Christ." Notice the order of things the Savior told the surviving Nephites to do, and what Moroni used in his final counsel to us in the scriptures cited above. Note that neither the Savior nor Moroni said we should "repent" or "deny ourselves" ("get things under control") first. Instead we first must "return" or "come unto Christ." We must first admit our mistake to Him, and many times this confession includes the bishop. Then, after confessing, we qualify for His grace to help us "deny" ourselves. Trying to "get things under control" first is not repentance. It is merely "relying upon the arm of flesh." It is merely covering up the sin, it is merely not doing the sin—it is not repenting. To repent, you must "come unto Christ" first, which many times includes confessing to the bishop.

If we first try to stop sinning before we "come unto Christ"—and the bishop when necessary—we deny ourselves not only of the full help of the Savior, but also the help of the bishop's priesthood power. Thus we not only bear the full weight of our sin ourselves, but Satan also can tempt us more easily not only with this sin, but with any sin. Prompting us to delay coming unto Christ with our confession, which many times includes seeing the bishop, is one of Satan's most effective ploys to keep the Spirit out of our lives as we delay repentance.

As a bishop, I had nothing but love and admiration for the humility and courage of someone who came in to repent. We are never more like a little child, like the Savior asked us to be, than when we repent. Adults sometimes think they're too cool, and that they're above making mistakes. Little children, however, readily admit wrong and ask forgiveness. We need to do the same.

It takes courage to admit you're wrong and to talk about personal, embarrassing things. But most bishops have nothing but the highest respect for this courage. Go see your bishop immediately, if you ever commit some transgression that necessitates your confession to him, to clear up the matter and to clear your conscience so you can get on with your life! When we "come unto Christ" first, we feel immediate relief and healing because we're following the order of events He established.

Now let me mention another aspect of this important principle:

Forgiveness. President Kimball taught that we need to build many reservoirs in our lives and fill them with spiritual attributes to withstand the droughts of testing and trials.[1] If one of our reservoirs is repentance, I believe the "heavy water" in this metaphor would be forgiveness. You must constantly forgive others to be able to **KEEP THE SPIRIT!** The Lord is plain about forgiveness:

> My disciples, in days of old, sought occasion against one another and forgave not one another in their hearts, and for this evil they were afflicted and sorely chastened.
>
> Wherefore, I say unto you, that ye ought to forgive one another, for he that forgiveth not his brother his trespasses standeth condemned before the Lord, for there remaineth in him the greater sin.
>
> I, the Lord, will forgive whom I will forgive, but of you it is required to forgive all men. (D&C 64:8-10)

I found it enlightening about our nature as "natural men" that of all the scriptures I used as mission president, the above scripture, D&C 64:8-10, was the one I used *far more* than any other. What was difficult to understand was the concept that the offended one, when he is unforgiving, has the greater sin. I'll never forget one occasion when the missionary and I were taught by the Spirit why this is so.

A missionary, distraught about a series of offenses he alleged his companion committed against him, came to me for counsel. As in all relationship difficulties, there are at least two sides to the story. After checking with other sources, including the other companion, I found that the first missionary had good reason to be offended. When I read D&C 64:8-10 to him and suggested that he forgive his companion, he replied he would—after he received an apology. After all, his companion was the one who committed the offenses. I suggested that we should all follow the Lord's example in the timing of when we forgive. He didn't wait until His crucifiers had a change of heart or had asked for His forgiveness before he said, "Father, forgive them, for they know not what they do" (Lk. 23:34). The missionary demurred. But when I read him again about the unforgiving having the greater sin, he burst into tears. "President, how can this be?" How can *I* have the greater sin, when *He's* doing the offending? I want to do what's right, but I just don't understand this."

I, frankly, didn't understand it either. But, happily, I had been silently pleading with the Lord for revelation so I could explain this principle to this great missionary in a way that would give him a change of heart. The Lord blessed me with one of those "Ah Ha" experiences with the Spirit that President Marion G. Romney described one time when he said, "I know I was inspired tonight, I taught things I did not until then know."[2]

I said, "Elder, please listen with your spiritual ears and respond with your heart to what we're going to discuss now. What would happen if you decided to take this great injustice perpetrated on you by your companion, and instead of seeking justice, you simply accepted it and truly forgave him? What would this do for your companionship?" He replied, "I guess it would make it better." "What would this do for you, personally," I asked. "It would give me more peace," he whispered, as I could feel the Spirit filling the room. I asked, "Do you remember anything in the scriptures happening like this to someone else? Do you remember some innocent person having terrible injustices forced upon him, yet he still forgave the perpetrators? "Yes," he said, as we both began to weep, "It was the Savior." "Yes, this was part of His atoning sacrifice, to suffer this injustice. And Elder, I believe that unless each one of us is willing to do the same, we will not fully be able to understand or accept His atonement. As such, we will not fully participate in it, and we'll deny ourselves its full benefit. In other words, if we don't follow His example, doing on our own level what He did on His level, we deny ourselves His atoning power and entrance into His kingdom. That's why not forgiving is the greater sin. It has the greater penalty of us losing out on receiving the power He offers to "come follow Me." The person offending needs to repent too, but he's on a more elementary level. He hasn't yet been offered the opportunity you have, that is, to turn the other cheek and forgive. But he, too, will have to learn how to forgive someday before he can enter into where the Savior is. You have the wonderful opportunity to participate in it now."

He did forgive his companion. They talked it out, and he found out that he was not totally innocent. They forgave and forgot, and they both came away far better servants of the Lord. They both came to realize that as you forgive what others have done to you, you begin to let go of all that has been hard to forgive in yourself. They also realized the truth of what Elder Marvin J. Ashton said: "Those of us who cannot forgive and forget break the bridges over which we must pass."[3]

President Kimball taught: "Since the Lord forgets when He forgives, certainly we must do the same. No bitterness of past frictions can be held in memory if we forgive with all our hearts. So long as we are bitter, hold grudges, and are unrepentant ourselves and unforgiving of others, how can we partake of the sacrament?"[4]

You must constantly repent of wrongs against others and forgive wrongs others have committed against you. Repentance is not merely eliminating the wrong, but replacing it with something right. It is not merely the discipline of exclusion, but the discipline of inclusion, plus the inclusion of the grace of the Savior. If you do not repent and forgive, you disqualify yourself from the ability to receive and **KEEP THE SPIRIT!** You therefore can't have the "assurance of things hoped for, the evidence of things not seen" (Heb. 11:1, JST) of faith. Orson Pratt observed that the Lord provides us with "evidences" to build our faith, but if we have excluded the Spirit from us through lack of repentance, we cannot discern them. Said he:

> It is often the case, that the judgment becomes so weak and beclouded [by unrighteousness], that the evidences, however great, and clear, and lucid, and demonstrative, produce no sensible impression upon the mind. Hence, faith does not always exist in the impaired or vitiated minds with a strength proportioned to the degree or force of the evidence.[5]

As you testified to your beloved investigators, I testify to you, Jesus Christ will heal you when you repent. You will feel immediate relief by doing it His way.

When Peter was walking on the water to the Savior, but started losing faith and began to sink, "he cried, saying, Lord, save me. And *immediately* Jesus stretched forth his hand, and caught him" (Mt. 14:30-31). Just as the Savior did for Peter, he will immediately stretch forth His hand for you too. But, as Peter, you need to call first.

As Elder Scott said in the October, 1992 General Conference, "Don't hit bottom before you ask for help." Be like Peter: cry for help before you start to drown.

Repentance truly removes you "beyond the barricade" to "a world you long to see" because you will "join in the fight that will give you the right to be free." "Come Unto Jesus"[6] first, and receive rest and strength through repentance, so you can

KEEP THE SPIRIT!

6

SEARCH THE BOOK OF MORMON — THE KEYSTONE OF YOUR RELIGION —

Feast upon the words of Christ.
—*2 Nephi 32:3*

President Benson said the Church in general, and those of us in particular who take lightly the Book of Mormon by not regularly feasting from it, are under condemnation of the Lord. He tells of four blessings we will receive by regularly searching its pages: (1) we will avoid deception, (2) we will resist temptation, (3) we will keep on the straight and narrow path, and (4) we will enjoy life in greater abundance.[1]

As their bishop, I was greatly alarmed at the casualness at which many RMs (who really knew better) regarded the Book of Mormon. Here is what my experience shows. Remember, these figures are the reading habits of only RMs who have been home two years or less, those who testified recently of the importance of the Book of Mormon on their missions! In my survey "*Near daily*" equals 26 days or more per month.

2% Read the Book of Mormon near daily about 30 minutes per day.

5% Read the Book of Mormon near daily about 20 minutes per day.

20% Read the Book of Mormon near daily about 15 minutes per day.

70% Read the Book of Mormon near daily less than 15 minutes per day.

3% Read the Book of Mormon irregularly.

Remember the "mists of darkness" that covered the straight and narrow path in Lehi's dream of the tree of life? These "are the temptations of the devil, which blindeth the eyes, and hardeneth the hearts of the children of men, and leadeth them away into broad roads, that they perish and are lost" (1 Ne. 12:17). All four of the promises mentioned above by President Benson keep you from being lost in these mists. The Book of Mormon makes it possible to keep sight of the tree of life.

How important is it to keep sight of what you really want and not have it obscured by the mists of darkness? Let me illustrate with a story from Joel Weldon.

> Florence Chadwick, at 34, had already set the record for swimming the English Channel both ways. Now she was attempting to set a record of swimming from Catalina Island to the mainland. But this 4th of July the ocean was an ice bath; the fog was so thick she couldn't even see the support boat; sharks had to be driven away with rifle shots. Hour after hour she struggled through the frigid water as millions watched on TV. Her mother and trainer encouraged from the boat, telling her it wasn't far and urged her not to quit. But after 16 hours of seeing nothing but a thick fog bank ahead of her, and not knowing that she only had a 1/2 mile to go (of the 26 miles), she asked to be pulled out of the water. Still thawing out her chilled body a few hours later, she told reporters: "Look, I'm not making excuses, but if I could have seen land I could have made it." It wasn't fatigue, cold water, or fear of sharks that defeated her, but fog—the fact that she could not see her goal. Two months later, on a clear day, she was the first woman to swim the channel, beating the men's record by two hours![2]

Searching the Book of Mormon keeps the real goal in sight. The way to turn reading the scriptures into "feasting" from them is by making the Lord a promise and a request. Promise that you'll spend X minutes a day (President Benson recommends that we spend 30) for Y days in the Book of Mormon. For example, promise you'll spend 30 minutes a day for 30 days. If this is too much, promise less, but make a promise. You not only gain much in will power and self esteem by making a promise (even a small one) and keeping it, but the Lord has commanded that "ye shall bind yourselves to act in all holiness before me" (D&C 43:9). The Lord works by commitments, and this is the way He has prepared for us to receive any blessing from Him. You must first "bind" yourself to do what you've promised the Lord, in order to receive your requested blessing (if it is His will).

Request the Lord to bless you with two things. Ask that, as a result of your reading, you may come to know Him better—not merely "know about" Him, but *know* Him. Also, ask that he bless you with some of the spiritual treasures that are buried in the pages of the Book of Mormon. I do not refer to the concepts and ideas that are there, as great as they are; these are intellectual treasures. Ask that the Lord bless you with spiritual treasures. These are taught to you by the Spirit. What is taught varies from time to time, and from person to person. When I've asked ward members to take the 30/30 challenge, I've requested they write me a note about what they learned. Among other wonderful experiences, the notes *all* speak of receiving the four promises of President Benson, with extra help in controlling their thoughts. From personal experience, and from the experiences of ward members, I testify that 30 minutes a day has great power to guiding and strengthening our lives.

The president of our university stake asked the bishops to be sure that ward members not be overly burdened with Church work to the detriment of their studies. I believe you can spend 30 minutes a day in the Book of Mormon and still keep this counsel. In fact, I agree with President Benson, you need this much to be balanced.

As a result of "binding" yourself to the Lord, you qualify for blessings which otherwise are not available if you only do the "works" but make no commitment. You have the "works" (reading the Book of Mormon) but not the "faith" (asking for the blessing). Just as "faith without works is dead" (Jas. 2:20), so works without faith aren't as effective as the two combined. After you've completed a time commitment on a promise, make another one. Keep making new time commitments until you've developed a habit so strong you can maintain it without making time commitments.

President Benson said we should "feast" in the Book of Mormon. This verb in Portuguese is "banquetear." A banquet is a grand feast held in the perfect setting, the attendance of which is anticipated with considerable relish. You make careful preparations, arrive on time, and wear the proper attire.

Can you imagine what your host would think if you showed up in pajamas, grubbies, or only your garments?! For the same reason, I believe your "banqueting" should include wearing proper attire, since the clothing worn affects your attitude about any occasion. I thus asked our missionaries to be fully dressed for proselyting when they "feasted." This shows the Lord you value this time to be taught by the Spirit and receive personal revelation. You don't go to the temple in casual attire.

Hayden, Bach and other musical greats said they only wore their best clothes when composing so they could feel comfortable in asking God for personal revelation.[3] The producer of the movie classic "Gone with the Wind" knew that what actors wear affects their performance. Among other expensive details in the costumes, he used two or three of the finest leathers in each pair of custom-made shoes and had petticoats made with eyelet ruffling, lace, and ribbons tied in little bows. When asked by one of the actresses why he was spending all this extra money on things that would not be seen on camera he replied, "Your father is the richest plantation owner in Georgia, and I want you to feel like a rich plantation owner's daughter."[4] What you wear does affect your performance in any activity.

When you go to a banquet you feast, you don't merely nibble. The difference between feasting and nibbling is the difference between what you did when you went to a member's home for dinner, or when your companion fixed "lunch." The same with the Book of Mormon: you feast (30 minutes), you don't nibble (a few minutes).

Like the location of a banquet, where you are when you feast in the Book of Mormon is important. You need to be where you can give total attention, and read with "a sincere heart, with real intent" (Moro. 10:4). You should be seated at a desk, if possible, not lounging in bed, reading during meals, or traveling. You can read during those times too, but don't count it as your 30 minutes of feasting.

The time that a banquet is held is carefully planned so that everyone can attend. Likewise, when you feast is important. If possible, do your feasting so you can give the Lord the "first fruits" of the day. (More on this in chapter eleven and its "Five Golden Rings.")

Stephen Covey teaches that the scriptures are a "divine interview," becoming a "check list on your spirituality."[5] If you find yourself slipping, and the scriptures start losing their appeal to you, gird up the loins of your mind and, out of duty (to begin with), get back to reading regularly. Duty will eventually restore the desire to read.

In order to maintain the desire to read, you must also live so the Spirit feels comfortable being with you. Your understanding of the scriptures will be in direct proportion to your ability to receive the Spirit. If you do not have the Spirit with you, the scriptures won't have any natural appeal to you. You will then prefer to read other things that are more "interesting" or "stimulating." The Lord will become a stranger to you as you begin to think different thoughts and feel different feelings.

It is easy to become confused by the pressures and aspirations of the "real world." As the Urim and Thummim helped the Prophet Joseph Smith interpret the correct meanings of the ancient records, so the Book of Mormon can become your Urim and Thummim, helping you interpret what the correct needs are for your soul, as it helps you

KEEP THE SPIRIT!

7

Be Clean
Live in the "Real" World, — Not the "Reel" World —

Thou shalt not . . . commit adultery, . . . nor do anything like unto it.

—Doctrine and Covenants 59:6

As much as you firmly believe in chastity of actions and thoughts when you leave the mission field, problems related to chastity jointly constituted the single most common reason why RMs would come and visit me, their bishop.

Sexual purity has a tremendous effect on receiving and maintaining the Spirit. But it is greatly misunderstood by young adults, and it is one of the top temptations Satan uses on them.

President Benson spoke out strongly against unchastity:

> One of the most sobering statements about being unchaste is that of Alma to his son Corianton: "Know ye not, my son, that these things are an abomination in the sight of the Lord; yea, most abominable above all sins save it be the shedding of innocent blood or denying the Holy Ghost?" (Al. 39:5). Very few of us will ever be guilty of murder or of the sin against the Holy Ghost. But the law of chastity is frequently broken, and yet it stands next to these other sins in seriousness in the eyes of the Lord.[1]

Jacob 4:13 says that truth is "things as they really are." Or, as economists like to say, things as they are in the "real world," not an imagined one. What is the truth about sexual conduct? First, let me give you the telestial (counterfeit) "reel world" concepts as promoted by Hollywood, then the "real world" Gospel standards. If it sounds like I'm being too serious, it's because I am trying to be too serious, or rather, deadly serious.

What we're talking about here is literally the difference between spiritual life and death.

Here are some comments RMs have told me to justify their sexual misconduct. They are typical of what the "reel world" of Hollywood foists on us as representative of the "real world." They are, however, things as they "reelly are," not how things "*really* are." Unfortunately, there are some RMs that have been fooled or lulled into buying into these deceptions (2 Ne. 28:8, 21):

"What's wrong with making-out or a little petting?"

"Why can't two people who love each other, people who are engaged, express their love and commitment to each other with some kissing and petting, especially if we don't 'go all the way?' After all, we're not hurting anyone else."

"As long as we have our clothes on and we don't put our hands anywhere we shouldn't, we're OK, aren't we?"

These comments are typical of Satan's "reel world" counterfeits of "real world" standards.

Here are the "real world" Gospel standards according to "things as they really are." "Thou shalt not . . . commit adultery, . . . nor do anything like unto it" (D&C 59:6). President Kimball defined "anything like unto it" as "petting"—or worse—and he says the thoughts and feelings that go on inside you when you're indulging in it as nothing more than "mental adultery."[2] My admonition to our returning missionaries was the same as that of Elder Gene R. Cook[3]: "You do not have the right to cause sexual arousal in anyone, including yourself, except your spouse." Therefore, if your intent is to sexually "turn on" yourself or someone who is not your spouse, you have crossed over the line into sexual impurity. This includes not only your actions, but your dress, your body language, your conversations, your letters, and anything else that has the *intent* of causing sexual arousal in yourself or someone who is not your spouse. Granted, there are different degrees of severity, but they are all still over the line. They disqualify you from the Spirit to a degree, and they require repentance.

Elder Gene R. Cook warned us this way:

> You have no right whatsoever to stimulate a woman sexually in any way, means, or form unless she is your wife. Let me say that to you one more time. You have no right whatsoever to stimulate a woman sexually by any means or in any form—any way—unless she is your wife. That takes in things such as conversations, looks, touches, and

> anything like unto it. In my mind, you begin to step on that line if you begin to violate that principle by sexually exciting some person [outside of marriage].[4]

Each one of us knows the difference between a kiss of love and a kiss of lust. A kiss of love is saying, "I love and care for you, I respect you." When you give a kiss of lust you are saying, instead, "I lust after you." In fact, you are saying even less than this. You are really saying, "I lust after your physical body so much, I don't care what I do to your spiritual body in the process. And as long as I can satisfy my physical body, I don't care what I do to my spiritual body either."

Appropriate sexual conduct cannot be participated in as a solo; it must be a duet, and only with your spouse. Remember, in the temple you made a covenant to have "no sexual relations," not merely to have no sexual "intercourse," with anyone except your spouse.

There's one caution that I want to warn you against, because this is what the RMs in my ward told me was a treacherous, well-concealed snare for them. By the way, when the scriptures talk about Satan's deceptions, they usually use the word "snare" instead of "trap." If "trap" is used, it is usually combined with "snare." A trap is a device to catch something. A snare is a trap too, but it adds an enticement—bait—to induce the hunted to come close enough to the trap to be snared. Alma, when he was contending against Zeezrom, warned us about Satan and his "snares" this way:

> And behold I say unto you all that this was a snare of the adversary, which he has laid to catch this people, that he might bring you into subjection unto him, that he might encircle you about with his chains, that he might chain you down to everlasting destruction, according to the power of his captivity. (Alma 12:6)

The snare to which these RMs are referring, that increases desire for sexual relations, is the viewing of R-rated movies and videos. And the bait in the snare that too many RMs have taken is this: "There's just one bad scene it it. It won't affect me that much." This is the 1990's A.D. version of what Nephi said in the 550's B.C., describing Satan's bait: ". . . there is no hell; and he saith unto them: I am no devil, there is none" (2 Ne. 28:22). I've had several RMs tell me that they've had sex scenes unexpectedly pop into their minds from movies they admitted they should have never seen, even while in the temple.

President N. Eldon Tanner warned us of this danger:

> We are surrounded by the promotional literature of illicit sexual relations on the printed page and on the screen. For your own good, avoid it. Pornographic or erotic stories and pictures are worse than filthy or polluted food. The body has defenses to rid itself of unwholesome food, but the bran won't vomit back filth. Once recorded it will always remain subject to recall, flashing its perverted images across your mind, and drawing you away from the wholesome things of life.[5]

Randal A. Wright did some interesting research with unmarried college and high school students.[6] He found a correlation between R-rated movies and the desire for sex. His results show that as the number of R-rated movies seen increases, the desire for sex also increases. He divided the students into four approximately equal groups, according to the number of R-rated movies they had seen during 1992: Group 1 saw 0 to 5, Group 2 viewed 6 to 15, Group 3, 16-25, and Group 4 saw 26 or more. Here are his findings:

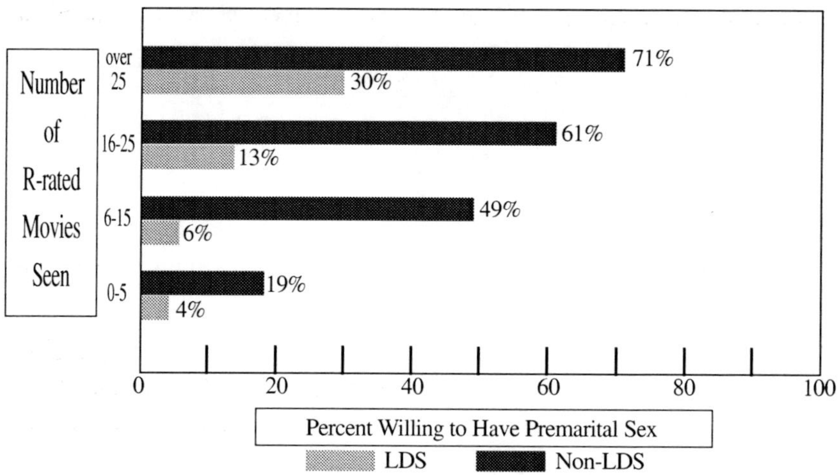

Notice the strong correlation between the number of R-rated movies seen and how permissive the student's sexual attitude is. The non-LDS high exposure group is 3.5 times more willing to have premarital sex than the low exposure group. But the LDS students are influenced even more: Those seeing the 25+ R-rated movies are willing to have premarital sex 7.5 times more than those seeing 0-5 R-rated movies.

I believe this increased level of temptation is because of the principle given in Alma 24:30:

> And thus we can plainly discern than after a people have been once enlightened by the Spirit of God, and have had great knowledge of things pertaining to righteousness, and then have fallen away into sin and transgression, they become more hardened, and thus their state becomes worse than though they had never known these things.

It's clear that R-rated movies and videos increase the desire for sex. This is also true of R-rated music, and especially R-rated music videos. Elder Gene R. Cook tells of returning from Mexico when Mick Jagger of the Rolling Stones sat next to him. Among other things during the 3½ hour flight, Elder Cook bore his testimony of the Book of Mormon, and Mick Jagger bore his testimony that, "Our music is calculated to drive the kids to sex. It's not my fault what they do; it's up to them. I'm just making a lot of money."[7]

By choosing to indulge yourself with inappropriate movies, you greatly increase the carnal desires of the natural man, as Alexander Pope observed some years ago in *An Essay on Man* (epistle i, 1.217):[8]

> Vice is a monster of so frightful mien,
> As, to be hated, needs but to be seen;
> Yet seen too oft, familiar with her face,
> We first endure, then pity, then embrace.

President Benson warned in no uncertain terms about choosing to see R-rated movies:

> "The lusts of your eyes." In our day what does that expression mean? Movies, television programs, and video recordings that are both suggestive and lewd. Magazines and books that are obscene and pornographic.
>
> We counsel you, young men, [this includes young women as well] not to pollute your minds with such degrading matter, for the mind through which this filth passes is never the same afterwards. Don't see R-rated movies or vulgar videos or participate in any entertainment that is immoral, suggestive, or pornographic.[9]

Remember, incorrect moral choices are rarely made intentionally, but by default. The most effective way to make correct moral choices is with a "provident promise." (See chapter thirteen, "Provident Promises.")

I would also suggest you read two of the finest talks on sexual purity ever given. They are "Of Souls, Symbols, and Sacraments" by Jeffrey R. Holland,[10] and "The Gospel and Romantic Love" by Bruce C. Hafen.[11]

You need to live in the "real world" and not be fooled or snared into following Satan's counterfeit ideas that a fallen, telestial, "reel" world has adopted:

> And there shall also be many which shall say: Eat, drink, and be merry, nevertheless, fear God—he will justify in committing a little sin . . . there is no harm in this; and do all these things, for tomorrow we die [or, as Bill Murray would say in the movie "Groundhog Day," "for I will live tomorrow over again"], and if it so be that we are guilty, God will beat us with a few stripes, and at last we shall be saved in the kingdom of God. (2 Ne. 28:88)

Live in the *real* world so you can

KEEP THE SPIRIT!

8

Honor the Sabbath The Key Day — to a Successful Week —

Call the sabbath a delight . . .

—Isaiah 58:13

Why is it so important to keep the Sabbath day, anyway? What good does it do me? My experience shows that many RMs stop considering the Sabbath a "delight," and echo a comment similar to this instead:

> I've been troubled by my lack of spiritual progress since my mission, and I attribute it in part to not keeping the Sabbath as I should. I'm sure there are other members for whom the Sabbath simply means going to meetings for three hours, not going to the store, not going to work, and on fast Sunday, skipping breakfast. I feel that there's a lot of confusion about the way to observe the Sabbath properly.[1]

Here's a quick exposition of "The Five Rs," some technics that will help the Sabbath to truly be a "delight" for returned missionaries.

Remember. It's significant that the Lord uses the verb "remember" in the Ten Commandments: "*Remember* the Sabbath day, to keep it holy" (Ex. 20:8). We all need constant reminders to keep us on track, but it appears that the Lord thought it necessary to use *one whole day* out of seven to help us "remember" Him. We remember Him by remembering His commandments, His blessings to us, His sacrifice for us. We remember the Sabbath by remembering our "oblations" (oblations means "offerings, whether of time, talents, or means, in service of God and fellowman." See D&C 59:12, footnote b). "But *remember* that on this, the Lord's day, thou shalt offer thine oblations and thy sacraments unto the Most High . . . ." (D&C 59:12). Partaking of the sacrament worthily not only helps you remember your baptismal covenant, but renews it, as well as renewing all other covenants you've made with the Lord.

Repent. D&C 59:12 continued: ". . . confessing thy sins unto thy brethren, and before the Lord." During the Sabbath, before Sacrament meeting, is an ideal time to evaluate your week. Decide what you need to repent of. Then, during the administration of the sacrament, in addition to pondering about His sacrifice, you can offer Him your sacrifice of a "broken heart and a contrite spirit" (3 Ne. 9:20), by asking the Lord's forgiveness for your sins. Recommit not to repeat those sins and errors.

Rest. "For verily this is a day appointed unto you to rest from your labors" (D&C 59:10). Give your physical body and mind rest from doing and thinking about worldly pursuits. Your whole being—body, mind, emotions, and spirit—will be renewed during the Sabbath by its proper observance. "Cast thy burden upon the Lord, and he shall sustain thee."[2]

In the October, 1991 General Conference Elder James E. Faust admonished students to keep their studying off Sunday.[3] Many have found this to be wise counsel. Arrange your affairs so you can do this too, then ask the Lord to bless you with better understanding and grades. When you combine faith (asking for the blessing) with works (studying other than on Sunday), you will receive the blessing. Many RMs have told me this.

The principle is to make the Sabbath a day of rest. If you use Friday night and all day Saturday as your time for dating and recreational activities, instead of getting your homework done, and then use Sunday as your study day to catch up, you're doing your "work" on the Sabbath.

Certainly it's not wrong to study and learn on Sunday. It most certainly is not inappropriate to study the gospel on Sunday. But what is wrong is to lose the resting, regenerating aspect of Sabbath-day observance by allowing the burden of school preparation to crowd out the spiritual aspects of proper Sabbath-day observance. It's certainly not pleasing to the Lord for you to stay out late the night before and then be tired and falling asleep in your church meetings, either.

Be sure and go to all three of your meetings on the Sabbath. I was surprised and saddened to observe that some RMs adopt the habit of only attending Sacrament Meeting, using the rest of the day for study or entertainment. Then they wonder why they lack the Spirit. Besides attending your meetings, use the Sabbath for serving others, learning more about

Gospel principles, resting, reading, writing letters, and writing in your journal. Don't use it for studying secular subjects and working on your college assignments, or working, or for being entertained (Is. 58:13-14). Remember, too, to fast with a purpose, as you did in the mission field on Fast Sundays.

Recreate. Read and ponder your patriarchal blessing, especially on the Sabbath. This will help you recreate in your mind's eye—or as Alma calls it, your "eye of faith" (Al. 5:15)—the "real you." By recreating the "vision of your mission" (see chapter 14), you'll better be able to pursue your potential. To help with this, evaluate the previous week. What went right, what went wrong? Decide what changes need to be made. This puts your life back in focus. Plan the upcoming week. Especially plan into your week the things that will improve the relationships you have with yourself, with Father, and with others (family, roommates, etc.). These activities generally are not big and time-consuming, but "small means [by which] the Lord can bring about great things" (1 Ne. 16:29). They'll be pushed aside or will slip through the cracks if you don't plan them into your week. This refocusing on "what's most important" on the Sabbath empowers you to truly put "first things first" during the week. As you do this, you are actually spiritually creating your life, one week at a time, before you physically live it. You are thus fulfilling the measure of your creation.

Receive. As you remember to honor the Sabbath and keep it holy, you are enabled to receive two singular blessings. One is divine protection against evil. As was observed in an *Ensign* article,

> In our day, the Lord has told us that keeping the Sabbath will help protect us against the ills of a world that is degenerating spiritually. In one revelation to Joseph Smith, he rephrased the fourth commandment this way: "*That thou mayest more fully keep thyself unspotted from the world, thou shalt go to the house of prayer and offer up thy sacraments upon my holy day*" (D&C 59:0, emphasis added).
>
> Here is a divinely inspired plan for protection against immorality, rebellion . . . and other spiritual dangers that threaten us.[4]

The other blessing is to have offered to you the "fulness of the earth." "Verily I say, that inasmuch as ye do this, the fulness of the earth is yours" (D&C 59:16). Along this same line, if we continue our hymn quoted above, it states that the Lord "will never suffer the righteous to fall."[5] What does the "fulness of the earth" mean? Here's an example:

In Utah on Sunday, grocery store parking lots are jammed with shoppers' cars, but not at Macey's Food Stores. Here, there is quiet, the bustle of the week stilled. It all began in 1962 when Walt Macey and a partner owned Save-a-Nickel Markets in downtown Salt Lake. One day as Walt was working behind the meat counter, President Joseph Fielding Smith, who was a frequent customer, came up to him and declared, "Brother Macey, I didn't know you were open on the Sabbath. I want you to know that I won't be able to patronize you again until you are closed on Sundays." Without waiting for a response, President Smith turned around and walked out.

"The moment," says Ken Macey, Walt's son and owner of Macey's, "brought everybody up short. Not long after, my father approached his partner saying he could no longer be open on Sundays. Since the two didn't agree, they divided their stores, with Walt's partner warning him, 'You'll be out of business in six months.'"

Walt's store was renamed Macey's, and his former partner ended up losing his stores. Joseph Fielding Smith called Walt. "I see you are now closed on Sundays. I'll be back."

"Through the years," Ken admits, "once in a while we've hit some rough spots. Once our bank even said they'd pull out if we didn't open on Sundays, but we stuck it out. My father told me, 'If you do what you know is right, things will work out.' They always have. I suppose if we were open on Sunday, it would be possible to make more money, but how much do you need to be enough?"[6]

Elder Charles Didier, quoting Elder Mark E. Petersen, said:

> The observance of the Sabbath is an indication of the depth of our conversion. Our observance or nonobservance of the Sabbath is an unerring measure of our attitude toward the Lord personally and toward his suffering in Gethsemane, his death on the cross, and his resurrection from the dead. It is a sign of whether we are Christians in very deed, or whether our conversion is so shallow that commemoration of his atoning sacrifice means little or nothing to us.[7]

Stephen Covey teaches:

> If you partake of the sacrament righteously, your soul will be filled and not hunger for the world's things and ways, and your perspective in life and your purpose will be regained.
>
> The Sabbath is truly the key day for maintaining a depth of consistent spirituality, and each of the other six days will be richer and

more productive because of honoring the Lord's day. If you have a question about what can and cannot or should and should not be done on the Sabbath, ask one question and sincerely answer it: Is it worshipful?[8]

Honoring the Sabbath will go a long way in helping you

KEEP THE SPIRIT!

— —

9

ATTEND THE TWO TS

Attend with all diligence to the tutees and thou shalt more fully keep the Spirit and thou shalt more easily find thy eternal companion.

—1 Degneronomy 2:3

The "two Ts" to attend are the temple and the 'tute.

The Temple

President Benson taught this about the temple:

> In the peace of these lovely temples, sometimes we find solutions to the serious problems of life. Under the influence of the Spirit, sometimes pure knowledge flows to us there. Temples are places of personal revelation.
>
> When I have been weighed down by a problem or a difficulty, I have gone to the House of the Lord with a prayer in my heart for answers. These answers will come in clear and unmistakable ways.[1]

Nephi's account of when he "arose and went up into the mountain, and cried unto the Lord" (1 Ne. 17:7) is a type and example for all of us to follow. We can follow it to receive answers from the Lord in the temple for even our thorniest problems. Nephi, a man of the desert who didn't have any experience with ship building, was required to build an ocean-going vessel that would have to sail half way around the world, making a voyage of over a year without going into port for repairs or supplies. He even had to trust in the Lord to show him how to build the tools! But the Lord, indeed, helped him solve these challenges.

I also testify that any of us can receive personal revelation for solving problems by temple attendance. I've found answers to family, personal, relationship, business, and research problems in the temple. I believe I've even had a "Nephi ship-building" experience. Some of the details to our fireworks design came to me in the temple. Our unique design, which is totally different to the way I was taught to construct fireworks and to any other design on the market, has brought our company a great deal of success. This would not have happened if it were not for our unique design. Veteran fireworks makers at first made fun of our design, saying that it would never work, that it was dangerous, and that they would never use our "wacko products." Now they are "believers," but still are astonished that our design works so well! They are especially amazed because none in our company come from generations of fireworks makers like they do.

Let me paraphrase Nephi's ship-building experience as it applied to my fireworks-building experience when I attended the temple and "pure knowledge flow[ed] there" and "answers [came] in clear and unmistakable ways."

> And now, if the Lord has such great power, and has wrought so many miracles among the children of men, how is it that he cannot instruct me that I should build fireworks? . . .
>
> Now we did not work the fireworks after the manner which was learned by men, neither did we build our fireworks after the manner of men; but we did build them after the manner which the Lord had shown unto me; wherefore it was not after the manner of men. . . .
>
> And it came to pass that after we had finished our fireworks, according to the word of the Lord, my brethren beheld that they were spectacular, and that the workmanship thereof was exceedingly fine (1 Ne. 17:51; 18:2, 4, *mais ou menos*).

Like Nephi, I believe the Lord can reveal to anyone how to build any kind of ship or object (even something as trivial as display fireworks), and arrive at any promised land, if we have the faith to ask for help in the temple, and if it is the Lord' will.

The 'Tute

Elder Boyd K. Packer has counseled all college students to attend Institute classes:

> Institute has its fun and games, and a course in courtship and marriage. Now the boy-girl chase becomes more exciting because they begin to catch one another. The percentage of temple marriages among graduates of seminaries and institutes is *more than double* the Church average. Do you need any better endorsement than that? . . .

> Parents and priesthood leaders, check on your college students. See that they attend institute.
>
> Years ago, I was in Arizona with Elder Kimball. He gave a powerful endorsement of seminary and institute to the members of his home stake. Afterwards I said, "I will be quoting you all over the church." He replied, "You do that. And if you can think of anything better to say, say it and quote me."[2]

Taking 'tute classes each term will give needed balance and perspective. President Kimball taught that secular knowledge compared to spiritual knowledge was like comparing the froth on the milk to the milk itself. He said we need to have both, but the spiritual is far more important, and taking an institute class will help provide this knowledge.[3]

President Benson counseled this about where to gain essential knowledge:

> There seems to be a decline in faith—faith in God as the creator of heaven and earth, the Father of our spirits. There is a decline in faith in Jesus Christ as the Redeemer and Savior of mankind, not just a great teacher, our elder brother in the spirit, the Redeemer of the world. And this institution will be a place where men and women can come and learn the most essential knowledge available to men in the world. (Seattle Washington LDS Institute Dedication, 29 October 1961)[4]

The 'tute socials, parties, and dances will help give you the proper relaxation to "keep on keeping on" when your studies and work get to you. The 'tute socials have the atmosphere to maintain the Spirit. In contrast, many other socials you'll find around do not promote the presence of the Spirit. In fact, they detract.

Attending the "two Ts" will help you

KEEP THE SPIRIT!

10

Work Hard, Work Smart, Work Tough

Daily toil, however humble it may be, is our daily duty, and by doing it well, we make it part of our daily worship.

—Brigham Young

Work is a spiritual necessity as well as an economic necessity.

—Spencer W. Kimball

Work hard = *work hard*; work smart = *work smart*; keep on working hard and smart = work tough. Thus, to work hard, smart and tough (tuf) is to work "hardsmartuf."

When you work—work; when you play—play, but don't mix the two. When you study—study, but don't have the TV on, don't be listening to music, don't allow a lot of social interruptions. Yes, take study breaks, but then give 100% of your attention back to the books. Understand, you will

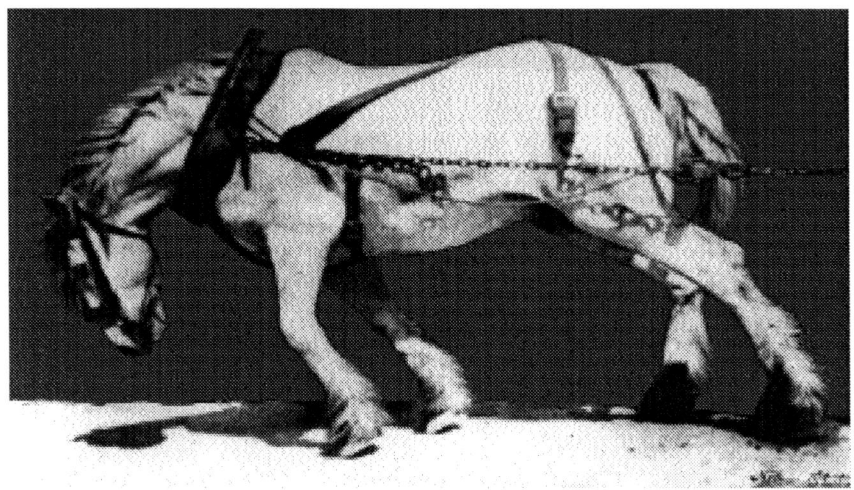

be competing against others who do pay this price, especially in upper division and grad classes, and in the work-a-day world.

I love the symbolism that the accompanying photo depicts of an old, blind work horse that truly is working hardsmartuf. He's not only pulling hard on his harness, but he also has on a bridle; he's being guided. And, he keeps doing this after many hours—or many years—on the job. You, too, must work hardsmartuf, using your own horse sense and especially the Lord's guidance to excel in the real world.

Here's a great statement from Hermain Cain, CEO of Godfather's Pizza, about working hardsmartuf:

> A reporter once asked me how someone could possibly live on a 40-hour-a-week minimum wage. "My father never worked just 40 hours a week, and neither have I," I responded. If you're only working 40 hours, you probably don't want to do any better than you're doing.[1]

Successful people are willing to do the things that unsuccessful people don't like to do and won't do. Successful people don't necessarily like to do them either, but they subordinate the short-term discomfort to achieve what they really want in the long term, and so they work hardsmartuf.

I didn't realize this fact of life until I was in medical school at George Washington University. I thought I had received tough training for competition by the strict mission rules. But my good Jewish roommate from Philadelphia told me he had been required to be up at 4:30 each morning to practice his violin, study the Torah and to do his regular school studies, all before he was off to school. After school, he worked in the family store. He had kept this schedule since he was eight years old! He received straight A's and was the most disciplined person I had ever seen. He told me, "You hicks from the West have no idea what work is!" Although this guy was out of balance, you will be competing against folks like him.

I flunked out of medical school after the first year, not yet having learned the work hardsmartuf lesson. Instead of studying, I chose to have the social time of my life, picking up the life-of-the-party nickname "Spanky," and seeking out the fun and praise I received by playing the piano at high-society parties for my landlord, who was a senior partner in a prominent Washington, D.C. law firm. When I told him I would not be returning because I'd flunked-out, he, being the out-spoken, hard-nosed counselor-at-law he was, gave me some free counsel. I still remember his exasperated look as his words and facial expression burned into my very soul. Said he: "Spanky, you've got to learn that there's a lot more to life than smilin' pretty and playin' the piano."

The Lord will bless you to favorably compete, and even better—to excel—but only if you "work like it all depends on you, and pray like it all depends on the Lord." Don't be fooled, as I was, into thinking you'll be blessed just because you're an RM and a member of the Church. You must also work hardsmartuf.

Working hardsmartuf also helps you resist evil. Remember the famous proverb that "an idle mind is the devil's workshop." President Faust said: "Work is another deterrent to evil . . . Satan selects his disciples when they are idle; Jesus selected his when they were busy at their work either mending their nets or casting them into the sea."[2]

You excel in the "real world" the same way you did in the mission field: you impose a determined, unswerving self-discipline on yourself to do the things that bring success and excellence, even if you don't like it at the time. One of these is the self-discipline to work hardsmartuf.

One of the keys to working hardsmartuf is the "one more" principle. Many of you encountered it in preparing yourself for various athletic events by lifting weights, running laps, doing wind sprints, or running "flights" (I love this term!) up and down the stadium benches. When the required number was finished, the coach always said "one more, one more." Generally you thought you couldn't do one more, that you had already reached your limit, and sometimes you were right. But the coach insisted, "one more, one more." He said this not because he thought you were lazy, or that he didn't believe that you had arrived at your limit, or that he enjoyed seeing you in pain. He insisted that you do "one more" because he knew—and so did you—that maximum growth comes when you force yourself to do "one more" when you really don't have the strength or wind to do that "one more." Even if you couldn't complete the final "one more," attempting to do so when you were already maxed-out was what brought the greatest growth. If you only did what was possible, you would only maintain the strength you had. You would experience very little or no growth.

To excel in the real world, you must do more than merely perform the possible—you must work at your potential. The possible is not your potential. If you only do what is possible, you will not receive the greater increase from the Lord to reach your potential. At best, you will only maintain the status quo.

Remember, if Beethoven only composed when he was feeling great and not suffering from earaches, we would not have that many of his masterpieces. It wasn't until after he was totally deaf that he composed his all-time masterpiece—the 9th Symphony. In fact, imagine what kind of world we'd live in if all the poets, writers, inventors, artists—or parents—only worked when they felt 100%. Here's a powerful quote from a letter written by one of our great RM's:

> My voice teacher taught me two very important lessons about being a professional. (1) To be successful at what you do you must give your whole soul to it. (2) Find an opportunity in everything you do. One day I came to a lesson congested and tired, and I told her that's how I felt. She said, "You will rarely find yourself in perfect condition to sing. Take this and make it an opportunity to learn what you can do despite your limitations. I always look at everything in life as an opportunity.[3]

With that, now follow this caution. Do not compare yourself with others. Work hardsmartuf at developing your gifts, your talents, at your speed, under the direction of the Lord. This is especially necessary so you develop at your correct speed and order. "Paced excellence" is what you want to achieve by working hardsmartuf, but not by running faster than you have strength (Mosiah 4:27).

Sisters, more than the brethren, it seems that you naturally want to be more diligent. You need to be especially careful not to attempt to "run faster than you have strength," and to not try to be a "Patty Perfect."

An important part of working smart is to make a wise decision concerning the career you will pursue. Ask yourself questions like these when deciding what career to choose. These are from Dean Burch:

1. What do I like to do?

2. Will it pay enough money to support the size of family I want to have?

3. Where will I have to live?

4. What training will I need: university, trade school, apprenticeship with a company?

5. Does this career have a place in the future or is it dying?

6. What kind of people will surround me?

7. What skills do I need to complete?

Here are fifteen key ideas that will help you in your quest to work hardsmartuf:

1. The kind of people you surround yourself with will greatly affect your philosophy of life. They can make or break you.

2. All success has a cost. Be willing to pay the price.

3. There are bad situations in all careers. If you don't like your immediate position, look into the future and see if things will change in four years. If you can see no change in your position in four years, then act now to change the situation. You're not a tree—move on!!

4. Be willing to make your own decisions. Pay the price for your decisions and reap the rewards of those decisions.

5. Put the blame where it belongs. The problem is not that the car costs too much, the problem is you do not have enough money to afford the car. Stop blaming other people for your problems. Take total responsibility for your situation.

6. Produce a high-quality product. Do it every month. Do it every day. Do it every hour. Do it every minute. The way to have a very successful year is to have very successful minutes. Each and everything you do counts at the end of the year or life.

7. You always get what you deserve, just wait.

8. Money is a result of good planning and execution of that plan, but your motivation should not be money, per se. It is only a reward and a tool.

9. Money is a by-product of service rendered. If you want a lot of money, render a lot of service.

10. Be worth more than what you are being paid. In tight times, the first people to be fired or laid off are the ones that are not worth more than what they are being paid.

11. Do not spend major time on minor things.

12. Better than having a million dollars is being a million-dollar person. You will lose your million dollars in a hurry if you do not know how to be a millionaire.

13. Do not be afraid to take a calculated risk. Life is a risk. Do not take a stupid risk. Risk can be either your friend or your worst enemy. Be careful but not scared.

14. Do not be afraid to fail, but do be afraid of not trying. There is nothing more pathetic than an adult that won't try.

15. These are my opinions based on my own experience. Seek out other opinions and compare them to mine. Then form your own philosophy of a career and competition in the "real world."

Remember, you can work hardsmartuf, achieving "paced excellence," if you

KEEP THE SPIRIT!

11

Prime Yourself to Start the Day Right — Five Golden Rings —

The first hour of the morning is the rudder of the day.
—Pascal

One of the major problems in large display fireworks is that some of the best effects are extremely difficult to ignite. To solve this problem, we coat these effects with an easy-to-start mixture of "primer" or "first fire." This, in turn, can fire the hard-to-light mixtures. It is similar to lighting a campfire. A match can't light a stack of logs, but it can light crumpled paper. The paper can't ignite the logs but it can light some kindling which, in turn, can ignite some branches; these then can fire the logs.

The idea of doing a low-energy activity, which then enables one of high energy to be accomplished, works well in the high-pressure area of professional sports. Priming brings an athlete into his "zone," meaning that he is so zeroed in on a task that he is oblivious to distractions. Bouncing the ball before serving in tennis or shooting a foul shot, or a batter swinging a bat as he waits for a pitch, are examples of spring-boarding an athlete into a high energy activity by first doing one of low energy. This low-energy primer works because it "clicks on" the athlete's mind to what needs to be done for a peak performance requiring high energy.

A great primer is a CTR ring. By merely looking at it, you're reminded of all the "right choices" you've committed to make in your "Provident Promises" list (see chapter twelve).

I also like to coat the shield under the raised CTR with a paste of water and black powder. This immediately turns the shield behind the CTR black, and the sulfur in the powder chemically turns the silver in the shield to a black silver sulfide within a day or two. It stays black unless you return the shine with some silver polish.

I like the symbolism of "choosing the right" by "clinging to the rod" (another definition for CTR) even though you're surrounded by the "mist of darkness" (1 Ne. 8:24). I also wear my CTR ring, with the letters facing me, on the little finger of my right hand. This way, it is as far right as it can go—good symbolism for making proper choices too.

Elder L. Tom Perry gave the following counsel about primers:

> I suggest that each of you find or create reminders to help you and your loved ones choose the right when the choice is placed before you. There is power in a tie tack, a CTR ring, or a white dress hanging in the closet if we associate them with our desire for purity and righteousness.[1]

Just as an athlete first warms up and primes himself so he won't go into competition cold, the "Five Golden Rings" are great priming since they warm you up for a successful day with the fire of the Spirit. Part of the reason people procrastinate is they don't understand that priming should always precede a big project or an important performance.

By the way, another great primer is to draw five small golden rings in the shape of the Olympic logo at the top of the page of your planner. This will help remind and prime you to do the right things. Here are the "Five Golden Rings" I believe will prime you with the "fire for the deed" so you'll give an "olympic gold medal performance" throughout the day.

1. ***Get out of bed early.*** Don't merely wake up. After all, it is a commandment (D&C 88:124). And note verse 124 says "arise," not just "wake up." Making the first thing you do that day a victory helps carry you through the rest of the day just a little ahead of the game. "There is a close connection between getting up in the world and getting up in the morning."[2] If you have to catch up on some sleep, take a short afternoon nap. Remember, sleeping-in is the first of the "Three Lil' Pigs."

2. ***Search the scriptures.*** Search especially the Book of Mormon. Again, President Benson has said each of us should spend "30 minutes each morning before you begin the day's work in reading the Book of Mormon."[3]

3. ***Counsel with the Lord*** (Alma 37:37). Do so through kneeling, meaningful prayer at least twice a day.

4. ***Ponder, plan and evaluate.*** Proverbs 4:26 says, "Ponder the path of thy feet, and let all thy ways be established." Two extremely powerful ways to *ponder* and "establish" are (1) making written plans, and (2) evaluating your plans, actions and accomplishments with the Lord.

Plan your week by taking about a half hour each Sunday or Monday to organize and write ("establish") the most important activities you can do in the coming week to progress in the three most important relationships you have—with God, yourself, and your family. Then, take a few minutes each morning to reconfirm these activities and plan the rest of your day. Ask the Lord's help as you plan your weekly and daily activities, and He will give you direction and guidance.

Evaluate, or as King Benjamin would say it, "watch" (Mosiah 4:30), your day with the Lord in your evening prayer. I once heard President N. Eldon Tanner say that the majority of his evening prayer was spent in evaluating with the Lord what went right, what went wrong, why, and how he could have done better with his thoughts, words and deeds for that day.[4] He's a great example to follow.

Evaluating is also a great aid in staying focused and having a better-quality prayer, even when you're tired at the end of the day. Next Sunday, before planning your new week, also evaluate your past week, and ask the Lord to help you make the necessary changes.

5. ***Make commitments to the Lord.*** Bind yourself to act in all holiness before the Lord (D&C 43:9) by making commitments to Him and to yourself about your written plans. "Commit thy way unto the Lord; trust also in him; and he shall bring it to pass" (Ps. 37:5). Read again in Chapter 6 about binding yourself to the Lord with commitments.

I want to emphasis the huge difference that evaluating with the Lord and "binding" yourself to Him makes in your achieving excellence. Here's a study done by a major university showing the incredible power gained by these two processes.[5]

Action	**Percent Probability of it Happening**
Hear an idea that you like.	10
Consciously decide to adopt the idea.	25
Decide when you will do it.	40
Plan how you will do it.	50
Commit to someone else that you'll do it.	65
Commit to someone else that you'll do it, and have a specific time that you will report your results.	95

As you can see from the above chart, when you "bind" yourself (commit) to the Lord that you'll plan and evaluate with Him at specific times, you almost guarantee yourself 100% success. "Binding" yourself to the Lord and evaluation are two extremely powerful—but often neglected—keys to excellence.

But where do you get the shot of spiritual adrenaline to push you to utilize these two golden rings? I believe the central ring is the Book of Mormon. Searching it faithfully gives this spiritual adrenaline. And just as the Prophet Joseph Smith first pondered the scriptures before he prayed, so too will studying the Book of Mormon prime you to pray more effectively and to perform the other "Golden Rings" that, in turn, will prime you to give your best performance possible for the day.

By doing the "Five Golden Rings" the first thing in the morning, you're offering the Lord the "first fruits" of the day and following Jacob's counsel before you start into the work-a-day world: "Before ye seek for riches, seek ye for the kingdom of God" (Jac. 2:18). Doing the "Five Golden Rings" helps you to worry less and to concentrate more on keeping your commitments and "staying in your zone."

How important is it to be primed well enough to stay concentrated on your goals and on the task at hand? Anyone who saw the 1993 Super Bowl can answer that. Dallas Cowboys defensive tackle Leon Lett grabbed the football as the Buffalo Bills' quarterback fumbled right in front of him. Lett took off for the goal line, some 65 yards away. No one was between him and a sure touchdown, and he had never scored one before! As he crossed the ten-yard line, Lett threw out his arms in triumph, keeping hold of the ball in one hand, of course. He never heard the Bills' wide receiver Don Beebe coming up behind him. At the one-yard line, Beebe knocked the ball from Lett's hand, ending the lineman's premature celebration! The "Five Golden Rings" prime you so you can better maintain your concentration.

The "Five Golden Rings" are prominent among the "small and simple things by which great things are brought to pass" (Al. 37:6). Doing small increments of the right things makes a big difference over time.

Here's an example from Joel Weldon. In professional baseball, a batter that hits .250 averages 3 hits for 12 times at bat and earns about $50,000 a year. A player that bats .333 averages 4 hits for 12 times at bat, but earns $500,000 plus a year! Does the .333 hitter earn 10 times the salary because he gets 10 times as many hits? Nope. Over a nine-inning game, each player is usually up to bat four times. The difference between the .250 hitter and the .333 hitter is only *one* more hit every three games! That's it! The one more hit every three games makes a huge difference—a half-million dollar difference![6]

The same principle applies with your actions and performance. Doing the "little things" makes a big difference over time, bringing to pass remarkable spiritual growth.

But even if it seems there is no visible progress, don't get "weary in well-doing" (D&C 64:33). Progress is being made. You may not see it yet, but you will. What is happening inside you is similar to the way bamboo grows. Even though most plants grow rapidly in Brazil, when a bamboo seed begins to grow, it can remain in the ground for up to five years before even a sprout appears! But then, watch out! It can grow up to three feet in 24 hours, reach heights of 120 feet, and be as strong as soft steel! What is happening during those five years is that the seed is sending out miles of roots to support the later rapid growth.

This is what you are doing too. You are preparing your mind and spirit and developing your own spiritual root system as the necessary foundation to support your future growth. "Wherefore, be not weary in well-doing, for ye are laying the foundation of a great work. And out of small things proceedeth that which is great" (D&C 64:33), but you need to "be patient until you shall accomplish it" (D&C 11:19).

You've "laid the foundation of a great work" in the mission field, both for the Lord and for yourself. Now, build upon it and continue to build your own miraculous future with the "Five Golden Rings" that will help you

KEEP THE SPIRIT!

12

WRITE YOUR OWN WHITE BIBLE — THE FOUR P'S —

This manual of essential instructions will be an important instrument for your mission. Use it as a daily reference guide. You will receive further instructions as The President deems necessary.[1]

Ah, the Missionary Manual, or as you more likely called it, the "White Bible!" Written and distributed by the Quorum of the Twelve and the First Presidency, this miniature booklet could fit in your shirt pocket, and it contained the rules and standards of missionary conduct. Although the "White Bible" was small, it was powerful since it also gave you direction and discipline. Those who followed it were far better missionaries than those who didn't. But when you returned back to the "real world" you didn't have this valuable guide.

But to really excel in the "real world," you need a guide just as much as you did in the mission field. If anything, you need it more. At least in the mission field, most everyone was going in the right direction most of the time. In the "real world" there are many people who don't have a personal sense of direction. The mists of darkness overcome them, or the people in the great and spacious building distract them, and they lose their grip on the iron rod and become lost. A "White Bible" for the "real world" would help keep this from happening. Here' a quote from one of our great RMs, commenting on what it's like to be home:

> I've found that while one is in the mission field and is being obedient there is literally nothing that can stop him. He knows when everything is going OK. However, here in everyday life the same principles are true, yet there are more forces that have the ability to confuse you.

> I've learned here just how important it is to be close to the Lord because I feel that the power of the enemy is even more cunning and more powerful here. It's strange, yet I sense that missionaries are somewhat protected, whether or not they're totally obedient, just because they are missionaries, (give or take a few of the complicated characters).
>
> As I struggle to adapt to my new environment, I find and feel more and more that one without a *defined* and *structured* set of standards that are *not compromisable* will surely fail.[2]

For the rest of your life, most of the problems and hassles you'll encounter will come from your not applying the guidance and discipline you learned in the mission field in the "real world." When you don't have to do something is the time you need to exercise self-discipline and do it anyway. If not, you will not achieve excellence in anything, and you will see others who have learned self-discipline receive what you wanted. A personalized "White Bible" for the "real world" will help give you the guidance and strength to do this.

There are "Four P's" that should make up your new "White Bible:"

1. your Patriarchal Blessing;
2. a "Provident Promises" list;
3. a prioritized "Values" list; and
4. a personal mission statement of your life's purpose or mission—a "Mission-Vision."

Write your "Provident Promises" list first because it is extremely important to have from the very first when you return home and it is easy and fast to do. Later, you can spend the necessary time on your "Values" and "Mission-Vision."

Your White Bible will give you the direction you need, but the strength to live your White Bible comes from frequently reviewing it. Like in the mission field, review your White Bible at least weekly. Unless you "have his commandments always before [your] eyes" you'll dwindle in unbelief (Mosiah 1:5), and unless you actually write your own White Bible, you can't review it. Here's another testimony to the vital importance of writing down what you want to live.

Brain Tracy tells of a study done at an Ivy League university about the effect of having written goals. The graduating class of 1952 was asked who used written, daily goals. 3% replied they always did, and the remaining

97% used them infrequently, or did not use them. In 1972 the survey was repeated and found that the same 3% were still using daily, written goals. But their net worth was more than the combined net worth of the other 97%![3]

Unfortunately, I've found that most RMs quickly lose this discipline of *writing* important things down. When I was mission president and had my final interview with each missionary, I asked each one to send me a copy of his "Promises" list within 30 days of arriving home. 100% promised me they would do so, but guess what percentage I actually received? About 7%! Interestingly, and I believe not coincidently, you'll notice that this 7% figure is also the same percentage as those who were diligently reading the Book of Mormon at least 20 minutes per day.

If writing is acknowledged as necessary for success in the "real world" of business, should you do any less for the even more "real world" of the truth, "things as they really are, and of things as they really will be" (Jac. 4:13)?

The Savior answered this question with the Parable of the Unjust Steward (Lk. 16:1-12). Elder James E. Talmage said this about the parable: "Our Lord's purpose was to show the contrast between the care, thoughtfulness, and devotion of men engaged in the money-making affairs of earth, and the devotion and half-hearted ways of many who are professedly striving for eternal riches."[4] And Elder Bruce R. McConkie added, "Ye saints of God, be as wise and prudent in spiritual things as the unjust steward was in worldly things."[5]

I'd suggest you make your own White Bible, patterned after the same size and style as your missionary one. It's easy, makes a fun project, and it will give added meaning to the contents. But if you don't want to go to this extra effort, that's OK. At least get started writing it on any paper! Putting it in your planner where you can always have it handy for review is great too.

Now let's go over briefly what you should have in each of the "Four P's" of your White Bible.

Patriarchal Blessing. Make a photocopy of your blessing. Reduce it as needed to fit the booklet or planner in which you're putting it. Read the paragraph in Chapter 14 about patriarchal blessings and include these suggestions too in your White Bible.

Provident Promises. This list consists of short commitments to yourself. This list of promises should include all the things you inwardly know that you must do, or must avoid doing, to **KEEP THE SPIRIT**! These are activities that you can jot down in just a matter of minutes. These are the things that your conscience keeps pressing upon you to do, or keep from doing. I'd tell our missionaries that in 20 minutes you can write the majority of your list down. You already know yourself well enough to know what you must do, or not do, to **KEEP THE SPIRIT**! There will be more about Provident Promises in the next chapter.

Personal Mission-Vision. This is a personal mission statement describing what you perceive and inwardly detect to be your specific purpose or purposes in life, your "errand from the Lord." You'll probably ponder about this for weeks or months, jotting things down as they occur to you before you can eventually get down what you feel can be a first draft. Then, one day, in a burst of energy and resolution, you'll quickly create the basic statement which will begin to guide your actions and goal-setting. Then you'll probably be fine-tuning this mission statement your whole life. It will be an exhilarating adventure of discovery, one you'll absolutely love! More about this in Chapter 14.

Prioritize Values. This will be another exhilarating voyage of discovery. Values work hand-in-glove with your mission-vision statement to give your life meaning and purpose. Whereas your mission-vision gives your life direction, your values give your life the foundation to work upon. The values you should pick are the same ones you cherished in your pre-mortal life and are taught here in this life by the Gospel. More on this in Chapter 15.

Writing and reviewing your own White Bible is vitally important for you to

KEEP THE SPIRIT!

13

MAKE PROVIDENT PROMISES YOUR OWN

— DECLARATION OF INDEPENDENCE —

The woods are lovely, dark, and deep
But I have promises to keep,
And miles to go before I sleep,
And miles to go before I sleep.

—*Robert Frost*

You found on your mission you were most effective in helping people change their lives under the influence of the Spirit when you used the "commitment pattern." In the "real world" you must also make "promises to keep" because you do, indeed, "have miles to go before you sleep." Making commitments to yourself and to the Lord is the way you are most effective in accomplishing anything.

There are some promises that are more effective than others. To illustrate these effective ones, let me tell you about the snowball fights we had when I was growing up. We built elaborate snow forts to defend ourselves, and huge quantities of snowballs were stock-piled to fend-off any attackers. We played a version of "Capture the Flag" in which we had the usual snowball fight but also tried to capture the other side's flag. These were great fun!

The competition was intense. To battle effectively, you needed a "Cool-hand Luke" for a look-out. His job was to see from where the enemy was really coming, distinguish a feint from a real attack, and keep watch even under a heavy barrage. If the look-out shouted the warning in time, the charge could always be driven back, but only with a heavy volley of readily available snowballs. You therefore had to make plenty of snowballs in advance, and have them easily available (not under some box).

Each side formulated new tactics and attack patterns to win the battles. However, no new weapons were developed. No new ones, that is, until I developed the "ultimate weapon" for a snowball fight: a snowball cannon. Although slow in firing, it was totally awesome since it was powered by acetylene gas. It could fire 3"-diameter snowballs up to a distance of a football field and could totally obliterate snow forts, leaving the other team exposed to our volleys of snowballs.

I expected my cannon to be the ultimate weapon for the whole winter. It wasn't. It was "ultimate" for about 22 hours—until the other side poured water over their snow fort, let it sit overnight, and thus developed the ultimate defense—the ice fort. An ice fort could defend against anything my cannon could deliver.

So, we found that in order to win the battle we needed five things: (1) an ice fort, (2) a 100%-effective look-out, (3) a large supply of snowballs, (4) having these snowballs readily available, and (5) a large, dependable team.

Now, how does all this snowball-fight analogy apply to "promises to keep" and the "commitment pattern"? We'll see this when we discuss items (3) and (4) above. They are the subject of this chapter. But first things first. We already discussed the first item in Chapter 4, "Control Your Thoughts." That's the key to your ice fort.

As far as the second item goes, the look-out, who in our lives, right now, is the only 100% effective look-out we can have? Right, our living prophet! Just like the look-out in our snowball battles, our living prophet can warn us where the attack is coming from (Al. 43:23).

With respect to the fifth item, a large, dependable team, as you **KEEP THE SPIRIT!** you'll stay on the Lord's team, and a more dependable or stronger team you'll not find (2 Ki. 6:16-17).

Now, let's discuss items three and four. What should be in our spiritual stockpile of snowballs? In order to be effective, snowballs not only have to be stockpiled, but available—easy to grab hold of and use. If not, the charging enemy will get through to our flag.

This is the fun part! I'm going to propose a method for making your moral choices in advance, before temptations concerning them confront you. This method can be used to take any idea and actually make it a part of you. You taught it and used it on your mission, and the General

Authorities use it. Robert Frost calls it "promises to keep." You know it as the "Commitment Pattern."

Advance commitments, or "promises to keep" based on truths in the scriptures, are the spiritual snowballs that you stockpile. Each promise is a snowball. As you found on your mission, it's how you turn "I'll try" into "I'll do." It's how you turn wishes into accomplishments. It's how you avoid temptation. It's how you can be "aware of the situation, but not let it change anything." (Remember Matt Bahr in chapter 4?)

The "promises to keep" that you'll need to make are correct "right/wrong" (moral) choices. These are the ones that will allow you to "keep his commandments." They also help you to "always remember him" and qualify you to "have his Spirit to be with [you]."

Here's an example from the scriptures on how making "promises to keep" makes a big difference when you're faced with adversity and you try not to let it change anything. It's the "Parable of the Ten Virgins" found in Matthew 25:1-13. Verse two says, "Five of them were wise, and five were foolish." The Greek translation says "wise" means "provident" and "foolish" means "careless."

To be provident means to be prepared, to think out beforehand what you're going to do in different situations. The wise, or provident, virgins thought ahead and prepared extra oil for their lamps, just in case the bridegroom was delayed. The foolish ones were careless and didn't prepare for this possibility. Elder Bruce R. McConkie taught that "the oil-filled lamps are symbolic of the Holy Ghost, and that the wise "have taken the Holy Spirit for their guide."[1] (See D&C 45:57.) Although this parable is mainly about watching for the signs of the Savior's Second Coming, it can also be used to illustrate how we should keep "watch" of our everyday lives and be provident.

One of the main reasons for many people's success is that those successful individuals are "provident"—they "watch" themselves and they make promises to themselves before they face adversity or temptation.

The way you make promises to keep yourself super effective, or provident, is to write down and review your promises. The more formal you make the occasion, the classier the paper they're written on, the more thinking you give them, and the more you review them, the more your promises will empower you to really do what you promise. As suggested in the last chapter, you may choose to put a copy of them in a new "White Bible."

There may be several things you think you're committed to that will not stand the test of stress, or will give way to rationalization if you don't write and review your promises. If you don't make certain moral (right/wrong) decisions in advance, in detail, and preferably in writing, you may not make the right decisions when temptations confront you.

Your promises give you more impetus to complete them when you write them in the present—not in the future tense. Example: "I search the Book of Mormon 30 minutes a day, every day." Not: I will search the Book of Mormon, . . . etc."

In order to make these promises part of your character, you need to rehearse them to yourself over and over again. Just as an actor isn't believable in the character he's playing on the stage until he's rehearsed his lines many times, you won't have these promises ingrained into your character until you've rehearsed them many times.

Remember, the attacking team "could always be driven back, but only with a heavy volley of readily available snowballs." Each time you say a promise to yourself, you place another snowball in your fort, and you make it more available. Not writing your promises is like going into the snowball fight with no snowballs. And not rehearsing them is like putting the snowballs under a box where they can't be easily reached. Rehearse your promises at least once a week—it makes a great Sabbath Day activity!

Incorrect moral choices are rarely made intentionally; they are made by default. In other words, you don't intend to choose wrong, you just don't choose right. Aesop's fable of the "Grasshopper and the Ant" describes this. The grasshopper didn't deliberately choose to go hungry and starve to death that winter; he just didn't get around to deciding to do something about storing up food in time. The ant, on the other hand, chose early in the summer to store food for the winter.

Make moral choices in advance, when guidance and good judgment are present. If you wait until a time of crisis, at the moment of greatest temptation when judgment is hazy due to mixed emotions, peer pressure or adversity, your thinking will be clouded. What you really want will be obscured. Writing the promises to yourself you want to keep and reviewing them often, helps you see them clearly, even in times of great stress. Because you write these promises in advance, you literally save yourself the effort of making these decisions over and over again throughout your life.

I call this your "Provident Promises" list because

1. you take the Holy Spirit to be your guide as you make this list;

2. it helps you be prepared for any surprises or stresses that would influence you to do things you really don't want to do; and

3. you have the aid of Providence to help you keep these promises.

Keep this list in your journal, or in some other private place like your new White Bible. List each promise only after you've imagined or role-played the most difficult kinds of conditions and circumstances you could face regarding it. Then review it frequently. It is a contract with yourself, a document of freedom. It is your own personal "Declaration of Independence" or "Title of Liberty" from the stress that comes from having to face repeated temptations and having to make the same decisions over and over again.

Your "Promises" list can be a spiritual health or life insurance policy. It shields you from incorrect moral decisions that can have such impact that you can become spiritually crippled from them for a long time, as did King David.

There are some situations that no matter how much will power you bring to bear, or how many good intentions you have, once you place yourself in the situation, it is impossible to extricate yourself. Here's a hiking example.

There is a spectacular area in southern Utah called Paria Canyon. There are "narrows," some four miles long and only 20 feet wide in some places, with canyon walls towering above you some 300 feet or more. Since Paria Creek flows through the canyon, you only hike when the water is low. In fact, a Bureau of Land Management pamphlet warns:

> Take the necessary precautions of being absolutely certain about the water level and weather forecast before entering the canyon. *Because once you enter the canyon, it is impossible to take precautions.*[2]

Just as you risk being killed by a flash flood if you place yourself in these narrows under some conditions, you can place yourself in great peril in certain situations that require a moral choice. The desires, appetites, and passions of the "natural man" are too powerful to be overcome once certain choices have been made. Previously made and rehearsed "Provident Promises" are the precautions you take before entering the canyons of the real world. There are some canyons you simply must not enter.

Making correct moral choices is not easy. But if you're not willing to expend the energy to write and review these choices in calm circumstances, as seen from the hiking example above, it's almost guaranteed that you won't have the strength to make the right choice in an enticing, energy-draining or hormone-packed crisis. In business, I've seen people give up their honesty to the lure of the dollar or "the deal."

When I was a bishop, every couple I counseled with, who wrote and reviewed a list of situations to avoid and a list of things to do, stayed sexually pure. But other couples who did not write, fell. The power of the pen is immense!

What kind of promises should you write? Any that require you to make a choice between right and wrong. They're listed in the scriptures. These choices make it possible for you to **KEEP THE SPIRIT!** and thus be your best self and live life to the fullest!

Some areas that are particularly helpful for RMs to make promises in are dating, entertainment and schooling. Here are some suggestions:

• *Promise that the person you say "goodbye" to at the end of the date will be a little better person than when you said "hello."*

• *Promise that when lights get low and thoughts are even lower, you'll be like Joseph and quickly leave* (Gen. 39:12). (As a bishop, I've heard some sad and scary stories of pajama dances, hot tubbing, and back rubs where the person felt uncomfortable but didn't want to cause any embarrassment by leaving.)

• *Promise you won't date anyone who isn't worthy right now to hold a temple recommend.*

• *Promise you'll not watch R-rated (or worse) movies and videos.* (The reason I make such a blanket request is that many an RM told me that they thought "R" movies and MTV would not really be "that bad." But they observed that the Spirit immediately withdrew from them.)

• *Promise you'll replace wrong thoughts with right thoughts.* (It's much like filling up a hole in the back yard. If you don't replace the dirt taken out with something else like cement, the first rainstorm fills the hole back up again with the same dirt.)

Take Elder Packer's advice and replace wrong thoughts by singing a hymn. Once my companion and I had to walk by Ipanema beach in Rio de Janeiro. When the "scenery" became distracting, I told him to sing a hymn. When he started humming "There Is Beauty All Around," I suggested another one instead.

One girl came to me about the problem of inappropriate thoughts. When I suggested that she think of a hymn, she replied, "But bishop, that's just the problem. I can't stop thinking of him!"

• *Promise to say no to fun when you really have to study or work that extra hour or two, or ten.*

• *Promise you won't go into debt for a new car.* Cars are only transportation—save until you have enough to buy them. And never go into debt for consumer items like computers, TVs, bikes, CD players, trips, etc.

• *Promise you'll listen to and heed the "look-out."*

• *Promise that you'll never let peer pressure make life's vital moral decisions for you.*

• *Make very specific individual promises that you'll not commit improper acts.* For instance, I will never drink alcohol, coffee, or tea, I will never smoke or chew tobacco. I will never take or smoke drugs. I will never cheat on my school work. I will never "neck," "pet," or engage in sexual intercourse until after I am married, and then only with my spouse to whom I am legally married. I will never fail to pay a full tithing.

• Also, *make very specific individual promises that you will accomplish certain significant goals.* For instance, I will obtain a current temple recommend and never allow it to lapse throughout my lifetime. Make moral decisions while you safely can decide your standards of conduct in advance, and record and review those decisions. Ask yourself, "What are my priorities, and is that the way I'm living?" Don't think that whatever is of concern to you will somehow take care of itself. "It" never takes care of itself, you do.

What you are doing with this exercise is striving to insure your success in the face of adversity throughout your lifetime. You make "promises to keep" because you "have miles to go before you sleep." Don't think that writing and reviewing promises is redundant, too insignificant an activity, or too simple to have much effect on your life and lifestyle.

Advance commitments to a predetermined course of action is the key to success. Olympic athletes, for instance, have certainly made and obeyed such commitments. So have those who have achieved success in their academic and business pursuits. What I'm recommending is that moral success requires a similar kind of advance commitment.

General Authorities have made such moral commitments, or "Provident Promises," because they know that "By small and simple things are great things brought to pass" (Al. 37:6). As President Kimball taught,

> Do not have to decide and re-decide what you will do when you are confronted with the same temptation time and time again. You need only to decide some things once. How great a blessing it is to be free of agonizing over and over again regarding a temptation. To do so is time-consuming and very risky and each equivocation may result in error. There are some things Latter-day Saints do and other things we just don't do.[3]

A way to make your Promises list even more effective is to make a contract with Heavenly Father. This contract involves a request and two promises.

Request that He prompt you, in an extra way that you can't mistake, the very moment you are tempted to break one of your promises.

In return, you first *promise* Him, just as you've already promised yourself, that you'll turn immediately from that temptation and "Avoid it, pass not by it, turn from it, and pass away" (Prov. 4:15). You won't believe the amount of extra help you'll receive when you ask Heavenly Father, with a promise, for this blessing!

The *second promise* you make is this: "If I do yield, I will speak to Thee about it on the very day it occurs." If you don't make this second promise, you'll possibly be tempted to discontinue your prayers because you feel you've failed Him by breaking a promise. There's no time when you have a greater need to talk with Father, and when He wants to visit with you, than when you are sick and need help. Jesus himself said he was sent to those who were ill, not to those who were "whole" (Mark 2:17).

Making a promise, even a very small promise to yourself, but more especially to the Lord, and then keeping it; then making another promise and keeping it; then making still another promise and keeping it, builds tremendous will power within you. You'll then be able to use this power to better keep your promises in the future and to serve the Lord, even under stress. Says Stephen Covey,

> Resist and overcome temptation, and you will absorb into your character the strength and fury of those temptations and be made that much stronger each time . . . You [thus] develop a reservoir of power, strength, and inner peace so that you are not policed by the opinions of others and your own fear of disapproval and hunger for human approval.[4]

Why make a "Provident Promises" list? Because you have "miles to go before you sleep." You need it to guide you throughout your life. Over the years, as your situation changes, a variety of different temptations will confront you. Your predetermined moral choices—your "Provident Promises"—will shield you from them. They will be your basis for righteous living. They are the "small things by which great things are brought to pass." They are your stockpile of snowballs. By reviewing them, you make them readily available, thus helping you

KEEP THE SPIRIT!

14

Catch the Vision of Your Mission!
Write a — Mission-Vision Statement —

To thine own self be true.

—Shakespeare

One day Alice came to a fork in the road and saw a Cheshire cat in a tree. "Which road do I take?" she asked. His response was a question: "Where do you want to go?" "I don't know," Alice answered. "Then," said the cat, "it really doesn't matter."

—Lewis Carroll

What's the use of running if you're not on the right road?

—German Proverb

If you don't know where you're going, you'll wind up someplace else.

—Yogi Berra

The road to anywhere is the road to nowhere, and the road to nowhere leads to dreams sacrificed, opportunities squandered, and a life unfulfilled.

—Thomas S. Monson

Each one of us is a unique person. Each has certain gifts, attributes, challenges, opportunities, and a mission to perform in life. This idea is expressed by Blaine M. Yorgason in his poem "The Monument."[1]

God,
Before He sent His children to earth
Gave each of them
A very carefully selected package
Of problems.

These,
He promised, smiling,
Are yours alone. No one
Else may have the blessings
These problems will bring you.

And only you
Have the special talents and abilities
That will be needed
To make these problems your servants.

Now go down to your birth
And your forgetfulness. Know that
I love you beyond measure.
These problems that I give you
Are a symbol of that love.

The monument you make of your life
With the help of your problems
Will be a symbol of you
Love for me,
Your Father.

The Prophet Joseph Smith taught Dan Jones that he had an "appointed mission" to perform. On the last night in Carthage, the Prophet replied to a question by Dan with the last prophecy he is known to have spoken: "You will yet see Wales and fulfill the mission appointed you before you die."[2]

Dan Jones had an "appointed mission" to perform. But does this mean that each of us has one too, or are they only reserved for Church leaders? George Q. Cannon answered this when he taught:

> We were selected and foreordained for our individual mission before the world was. And we had our parts allotted to us in this mortal state of existence as our Savior had his assigned to him.[3]

And Elder H. Burke Peterson said:

> Do you think for a moment that Heavenly Father would have sent one of His children to this earth by accident, without the possibility of a significant work to perform? Not just a few of you, but all of you. There are things for each of you to do that no one else can do as well as you. If you do not prepare to do them, they will not be done. Your mission is unique and distinctive for you. Please do not make anoth-

er have to take your place. He or she can't do it as well as you can. If you will let Him, I testify that our Father in Heaven will inspire you to know your special purpose here.[4]

Viktor Frankl, author of *Man's Search for Meaning* and a survivor of the Nazi death camps, recognized the concept of a specific mission in life for each person. He wrote,

> Everyone has his own specific vocation or mission in life; everyone must carry a concrete assignment that demands fulfillment. Therein he cannot be replaced, nor can his life be repeated. Thus, everyone's task is as unique as is his specific opportunity to implement it.[5]

Frankl believes your mission is not invented by yourself, but rather inwardly "detected."[6] Thus, because of the light of Christ, our conscience, each one of us can have an inner awareness of our own uniqueness, of our own particular mission. The lines, "My life has a plan, my life has a purpose," in the Primary song *I Will Follow God's Plan*, give the same idea.[7]

To help you better understand your life's mission, let's compare life to a football game. The objective of the game of life wasn't even known until the Prophet Joseph Smith ushered in the Restoration! Players wandered around the field, not knowing the objective of the game, at a loss of what to do with the ball. Can you imagine being a player in such a "game"?!

But with the Restoration, you understand you're on the playing field for two reasons: *First*, all players have the overall objective of learning to play football according to the rules and to run the plays well enough to make touch-downs, all the while adjusting to their new uniforms and pads. In other words, all players of the game of life have the overall objective of learning how to live life by giving obedience to God while in a physical body so they can inherit "immortality and eternal life." *Second*, each player has the specific objectives of learning what his part is in the plays, at a performance level which measures up to The Coach's expectations.

You, individually, and the team as a whole, couldn't be effective at scoring touch-downs—the objective of the game—until you found out that this was the game's purpose. Your particular position on the team is your foreordained or foredesignated mission. You can't be effective at your mission on earth until you find out what it is.

Your challenge is to learn what your particular position is, determine what is expected of you at that position, and then to do so as early in the game as possible. If you don't find out, you'll feel mighty embarrassed and regretful if you're replaced during the game, or if you never learn to play your position effectively so you're not invited to the post-game victory party. As Whittier said, "Of all sad words of tongue or pen, the saddest are these: 'It might have been.'"[8] After all, you did agree to do this in the locker room before the game. President Kimball taught,

> . . . in the world before we came here, faithful women were given certain assignments while faithful men were foreordained to certain priesthood tasks. While we do not now remember the particulars, this does not alter the glorious reality of what we once agreed to.[9]

Said Orson Hyde,

> Then, if it be true that we entered into a covenant with the powers celestial, before we left our former homes, that we would come here and obey the voice of the Lord, through whomsoever he may speak . . . it is not impossible that we signed the articles thereof with our own hands, which articles may be retained in the archives above, to be presented to us when we rise from the dead, and be judged out of our own mouths, according to that which is written in the books.[10]

You need to know which position The Coach has planned for you in His "play book." The Coach will tell you, but only if you are willing to search diligently. Searching for and detecting your specific mission in life will be a mind-expanding, exhilarating, and "most excellent adventure"! President Benson said this about the importance of fulfilling your foreordained mission in these latter days:

> For nearly six thousand years, God has held you in reserve to make your appearance in the final days before the Second Coming of the Lord. God has saved for the final inning some of his strongest children. There has never been more expected of the faithful in such a short period of time as there is of us. Each day we personally make many decisions that show where our support will go. What remains to be seen is where each of us personally, now and in the future, will stand in this fight—and how tall we will stand. Will we be true to our last-days, foreordained mission?[11]

Each of us, like the Bible's Queen Esther, has a special mission, "And who knoweth whether thou art come to the kingdom for such a time as this" (Est. 4:14).

We all know the overall objective of our life is to prepare to receive "immortality and eternal life" (Moses 1:39). But what is *your* specific objective, "your special purpose here?" The single most effective strategy of finding out what is in The Coach's "Play Book" is writing a personal mission statement, or as I prefer to call it, "a vision of my mission," or a "mission-vision."

Among the best sources of information on writing a personal mission statement are the two books by Stephen R. Covey: *The 7 Habits of Highly Effective People*,[12] and *First Things First*.[13] For some great insights into the art of writing mission statements, read both of them.

Stephen Covey teaches that mission statements give you security, guidance, and power: *security* because you won't be threatened by comparisons, change, or criticisms; *guidance* to help you make wise decisions; *power* to communicate and cooperate effectively, even under conditions of stress and fatigue, as well as power and ability to make hard choices.

Once you find your purpose—your mission—then catch the vision of it! Going through life without a mission-vision is like trying to solve a jig saw puzzle without its picture. "Where there is no vision, the people perish" (Prov. 29:18). A vision of your mission helps you see and organize all the activities that go on around you into fulfilling that mission. It's just like seeing ads for tire sales when you need new tires; the ads have always been there, it's just that you notice them now that you're on the lookout for tires. Thus, knowing what your mission is brings serendipity (accidental fortuitous events) into being, as you take advantage of these events.

Shakespeare understood this concept when he had Brutus say, in *Julius Caesar* (IV, 3):

There is a tide in the affairs of men
Which, taken at the flood, leads on to fortune;
Omitted, all the voyage of their life
Is bound in shallows and in miseries.
On such a full sea are we now afloat,
And we must take the current when it serves
Or lose our ventures.

A mission-vision is a written creed with two basic parts:

1. *What you want to be*: what character strengths you want to develop, what virtues or qualities you want to have.

2. *What you want to do*: what you want to accomplish, what you feel you're supposed to be doing with your life.

Mission-visions have been around a long time. The most famous one for we Latter-day Saints is Moses 1:39. Another well-known mission statement was given to us by President Kimball who said the mission of the Church was three-fold: preach the Gospel, perfect the Saints, redeem the dead. The Constitution of the United States of America is another example. In fact, Thomas Jefferson said, "Our peculiar security is in the possession of a written constitution."

A mission-vision isn't something you write overnight. It takes prayer, meditation, introspection, and self-analysis to produce the final form. It may take several weeks, even months, before you are comfortable with it. A mission-vision is a compass on which you build your life and base your major decisions. It gives you a sense of unique identity. A mission-vision should be a focus statement of what you want to achieve and be. But it is not a blueprint on how to achieve it. That is another project.

Writing, even attempting to write (but not merely thinking about it), does two things: (1) it clarifies your objectives because you are forced to think about what is really important to you, and (2) it gives you a real sense of commitment to then conduct your behavior in a manner congruent with your beliefs. As you do, others begin to see you are not being tossed about by everything that happens to you. You have a vision of your mission, and you are excited about it. When you're living your mission you feel "in sync," you feel you have your "act together" and that "all the pieces of the puzzle fit together." By increasing the clarity of your mission and your commitment to fulfill it, you also begin to change. In many cases you actually create your circumstances.

The process of writing is as important as the product.

Every person will live his life by either design or default. Life doesn't happen to you, it happens from you. Many people default their choices because they drift into those someone else has already made. They take the path of least resistance, or one that is the best known or least threatening at the time.

You need to start from where you are, with what you are—including your weaknesses—and then have the courage to risk Robert Frost's advice in "The Road Not Taken." Here are the last three lines.

> Two roads diverged in a wood, and I—
> I took the one less traveled by,
> And that has made all the difference.

Here are some ideas to bring to the surface those things that are still inside you. Plan to take a few hours for your first session, and then more hours over the next several weeks. This isn't a quick-fix project. This makes a great Sabbath activity.

1. *Find your own "Sacred Grove."* It need not be outside, although that might be ideal, but it should be a place where you can go to, to be alone and to think. Here you can listen to your thoughts. Of all living things, only humans can think about their thoughts. You therefore are larger than your thoughts and habits. You can stand apart from your habits and look at yourself. You can take charge and plan, as you counsel with the Lord, the kind of changes you want to effect in your life to be able to discern and live your mission. You also should listen to your conscience to discern what values are important to you and how they should govern your life. Meditate, and search the scriptures. Feast upon the words of Christ; for they "will tell you all things what ye should do" (2 Ne. 32:3).

2. *Use your Patriarchal Blessing.* This is your own personal scripture about your life's mission and foreordination. Read it weekly. Have it with you as much as possible. Also, make another copy and have it with your scriptures.

Analyze it, dissect it. A good way to do this is to take a sheet of paper and draw a line down the middle. At the top of one side write "Blessings," on the other side write "Warnings." Write down the blessings and warnings in the appropriate column as you come to them. On another sheet list your gifts, strengths, or talents it mentions; write what it says about roles, vocation(s), callings, duties or leadership; note anything said about family.

Your blessing will gradually reveal its fullest meanings, little by little, "line upon line, precept upon precept." But you must ask, seek, knock, look, and ponder with persistence and patience to fully plumb the depths of meaning of your Patriarchal Blessing.

3. *Expand your perspective*, as Stephen Covey says, by living out of your imagination, not your memory.[14] The best way to predict your future is to create it. Use the tremendous visualizing power of your brain. See the future with your mind's eye, or as Alma calls it, your "eye of faith" (Al. 5:15-18). Ask yourself what you will want to have accomplished by your 10th, 25th, and 50th wedding anniversaries. What will you want to be known for by your family, neighbors, community, and by those in your profession?

Before the Lord created the earth physically, he created it spiritually. What you are doing is spiritually creating your future. Nothing happens physically before it happens spiritually. If you do it according to the Lord's will, it will come to pass.

4. *Make a "Gift List."* We're all fairly average in most areas, but each of us has been blessed with enhancement in several attributes. These are unique to us. If we develop these gifts, we'll become excellent in them, far above average. Those who are happy are those who find these key areas. They concentrate and focus their energy on developing the successful fulfillment of these special skills. I also believe that the development of them is crucial to the successful fulfillment of your mission, and to your exaltation.

Your little niche of excellence is right within you or close by. Sometimes it is like a diamond—not recognized immediately until it is polished, processed and refined. Find your diamonds by asking: What things am I good at? What is easy for me to do? What do I enjoy doing most? What things am I the most competent or confident doing? What are my physical, social, intellectual, and spiritual gifts? Get rid of self-doubts, and list your gifts!

5. *Counsel with the Lord.* The Coach knows you completely. He knows your position on the team, what your purpose is, and how you can fulfill it. But he knows the only way you can develop is to detect your mission by doing a lot of asking and seeking. After all, he did say and promise, "Ask, and ye shall receive" (D&C 4:7).

6. *Seek advice from others.* Shakespeare describes this idea in an interesting dialogue in *Julius Caesar* (I,2):

Cassius: Tell me, good Brutus, can you see your face?
Brutus: No, Cassius; for the eye sees not itself
But by reflection, by some other things.
Cassius: 'Tis . . . very much lamented, Brutus,
That you have no such mirrors
as will turn
Your hidden worthiness into your eye . . .
And since you know you cannot see
So well as by reflection, I,
your glass [mirror]
Will modestly discover to yourself
That of yourself which you
yet know not of.

Many times other people can see character traits and gifts in you "which you yet know not of." It is necessary, however, to find mirrors that are straight and true. "Carnival" mirrors that are crooked or warped will reflect untrue and possibly harmful images of yourself. Don't accept all the advice offered; weigh it carefully with what you already believe about yourself.

Yes, you can know the contents of the "The Play Book." The Lord will show you, but that knowledge comes by effort and by putting into writing all you can learn about the individual you are and your special mission. You must strive to know yourself the same way God knows you—a unique individual, one of his children, one with unique contributions to make to mankind.

If you are not willing to expend the minimal energy to write down your insights, you really don't have enough desire to find out what's in "The Play Book." Emerson warned that too many are "always getting ready to live, but never living."[15] And as the hymn says, "Let each man learn to know himself; To gain that knowledge let him labor."[16] Paul said to "work out your own salvation" (Phil. 2:12). You need to work to find your niche.

A poem from Joel Weldon expresses your uniqueness[17]:

Every single blade of grass
And every flake of snow
Is just a wee bit different,
There's no two alike you know.

From something small like grains of sand
To huge gigantic stars,
Each one was made with this in mind,
To be just what they are.

How foolish to imitate,
How useless to pretend,
When each one of us comes from a mind
Whose ideas never end.

There will only be just one of me
To show what I can do,
And likewise you should feel very proud,
There's only one of you.

Columbus is an example of one who did what he felt he was inspired to do and be, especially of living out of his imagination, as well as his memory, and of counseling with the Lord. He wrote,

> From my first youth onward, I was a seaman and have so continued until this day. The Lord was well disposed to my desire and bestowed upon me courage, understanding and knowledge of seafaring. He gave me in abundance understanding of geometry and astronomy. Further, He gave me joy and cunning in drawing maps and thereon cities, mountains, rivers, islands, and harbors, each in its place. I have seen and truly have studied all books and cosmographies, histories and chronologies for which our Lord with provident hand unlocked my mind, set me upon the seas and gave me fire for the deed. Those who heard of my enterprise called it foolish, mocked me and laughed, but who can doubt but that the Holy Ghost inspired me.[18]

When you make decisions and conduct your life around a mission-vision, the Lord does indeed give you "fire for the deed" and inspire you to succeed.

The principle of discovering your life's mission and then spiritually creating a vision of your mission applies also to the main activities in the several seasons of your life. You should write a miniature version of a mission-vision for each major undertaking you'll do throughout your life. You should especially write one for your profession(s). Then write the values you need to develop and the goals you'd like to accomplish in each of these areas, based on your mission-visions. You thus have a main, overarching life's mission, one for your profession(s), and several smaller mini-missions (D&C 71:3).

President Benson taught that one or more of our mini-missions is (are) the profession(s) we have:

> It has been said that no one is born into this world whose work is not born with him or her. We bring from our pre-existent state various talents and abilities. It is our responsibility to strive to find where we can make a contribution to our fellowman—an area where we have some interest and abilities and where we can, at the same time, provide for our own.[19]

Those who create a mission-vision for a certain profession, but then wind up doing something else instead, have not wasted their efforts. The process of going for their original goal gave them experience and exposure to different options, opportunities and growth.

It's better to keep moving, change direction if necessary, even fail while trying, than to do nothing. The value of anything is not what you get from it, but what it costs you. Wisely said, "Far better it is to dare mighty things, to win glorious triumphs, even though checkered by failure, than to take rank with those poor spirits who neither enjoy much nor suffer much, because they live in the gray twilight that knows not victory nor defeat."[20]

A story from Emmett Smith illustrates the above concept. A young boy was quite gifted at playing the piano. By the time he was nine, he decided his mission in life was to be a world-renowned concert pianist. Lots of people play the piano, but there are few world-class performers. Many people scoffed at this "unrealistic" goal, but he persisted. His mother, a widow, took a second job; he went to work as a newspaper boy, and there was much self-denial from them both so he could take special lessons. He practiced hard, he and his mother sacrificing much over the next several years for his goal.

When he was about 17 and ready to make his debut, his mother died. This necessitated that he quit taking lessons and get a job to support himself. He had to give up his dream. All those lessons, sacrifice, and extra effort had gone to waste, many said. "See, don't set goals like that; don't set goals that are so unrealistic you can't achieve them and waste all that effort and money, only to wind up disappointed."

That man did not become a concert pianist; he failed. Instead, he became president of the United States. He was Harry S. Truman. And he used all that diligence and discipline he learned from practicing the piano those many hours over those many years; he used all those good work habits and the ability to sacrifice he acquired from working extra to become that great statesman and president.[21] Sometimes "failure" can lead us into other directions that make us even more successful than the one we originally started.

But sometimes, no matter how much we'd like to, we're not even given the opportunity to attempt a certain mission, let alone "fail" at it. We then need to regroup and rethink what we ought to be doing instead. Janet G. Lee gives a wonderful story about this.

> When my daughter Stephanie was five years old, I took her to register for kindergarten. When we arrived a teacher was sitting just

> outside the room with a box of crayons and several sheets of blank paper. Stephanie was asked to choose her favorite color and write her name. "She could write all the names in our family," I thought to myself. But Stephanie just stood there.
>
> The teacher repeated the instructions, and again my daughter stood still, staring blankly at the box of crayons with her knees locked and hands behind her back. The teacher asked once more, "Stephanie, choose your favorite color, dear, and write your name on this piece of paper." I was about to come to my daughter's aid when the teacher kindly said, "That's ok; we'll help you learn to write your name when you come to school this fall . . . ."
>
> On the way home I asked as nonchalantly as possible why she had not written her name. "I couldn't," she replied. "The teacher said to choose my favorite color, and there wasn't a pink crayon in the box!"
>
> . . . How many times are we, as Heavenly Father's children, immobilized because the choice we had in mind for ourselves just isn't available to us, at least not at the time we want it? I may not have all the colors of crayons that I want—but I do have all the colors that I need.[22]

Perhaps Father is like that teacher. He may have taken out all of the light-colored crayons—the yellow, pink, silver, white, etc.—so we could see clearly how well we write our name, and where we need improvement. Father knows what colors of crayons are best for us to use; and we need to find out what they are.

Elder John H. Groberg taught,

> In the past I have tried to figure out whether I should go into business or into teaching or into the arts or whatever. As I have begun to proceed along one path, having more or less gathered what facts I could, I have found that if that decision was wrong or was taking me down the wrong path—not necessarily an evil one, but one that was not right for me—without fail, the Lord always let me know just this emphatically: "That is wrong; do not go that way. That is not for you!" On the other hand, there may have been two or three ways that I could have gone, any one of which would have been right and would have been in the general area providing the experience and means whereby I could fulfill the mission the Lord had in mind for me. Because he knows we need the growth, he generally does not point and say, "Open that door and go twelve yards in that direction; then turn right and go two miles . . ." But if it is wrong, he will let us

know, we will feel it for sure. I am positive of that. So rather than saying, "I will not move until I have this burning in my heart, let us turn it around and say, "I will move unless I feel it is wrong; and if it is wrong, then I will not do it." By eliminating all of these wrong courses, very quickly you'll find yourself going in the direction that you ought to be going, and then you can receive the assurance: "Yes, I'm going in the right direction. I'm doing what my Father in Heaven wants me to do because I'm not doing the things he does not want me to do." And you can know that for sure. That is part of the growth process and part of accomplishing what our Father in Heaven has in mind for us."[23]

Now let me give a bad example of myself, who instead of taking the time and energy to prayerfully meditate about what I should do for my life's profession, or about my major in college, I based my decisions on false values, which led to disaster. I was even an RM and should have been familiar with decision-making and revelation when these incidents happened.

I thought I wanted to be a physician since I was young. But I should have realized this was merely wishful thinking when a girl I was going with, a daughter of a physician, asked me, "Why do you want to be a doctor?" I remember thinking that was the dumbest question I ever heard. But my reply was even more stupid: "Who wouldn't want to be a doctor and have all that money and prestige. Then I'll have the time and money to enjoy the important things of life." I still remember the pitiful look she gave me. She soon wisely terminated our dating relationship.

Did I really know what the "important things of life" were? I soon had the chance to list them. As I was going through the painful process of breaking up with another girl she asked me, "What is it you really want to do with your life?" Why do I go with girls that ask such dumb questions, I thought. But to this irritating question all I could reply was, "I want to appreciate the beauties of nature; to listen to inspiring music." That's it—that's all I could come up with! She replied, "Maybe you have to have your brother come home from his mission in a coffin to know what really is important."

So I went blissfully, but naively, off to medical school. A year later I was morosely sitting in the dean's office, after receiving an "F" in biochemistry and a "D" in microbiology. The dean asked me the same dumb question (this time in the past tense), "Why did you want to become a doctor?" When I gave him the same "money and prestige" answer, he replied, "I thought so. That's why you failed. Money and prestige can't give you the desire and energy to 'keep on keeping on' when your studies, time, fatigue, and outside interests crunch together. You had one of the top MCAT scores in the nation. You are bright, and you could have made it, *if* you had been in medical school for the right reasons."

This good man was a former stake president and knew just what questions to ask. He said, "You're a returned missionary, aren't you?" "Yes, sir," I replied. "So I imagine you've had some experience in counseling with the Lord in prayer, haven't you?" "Yes, sir." "Did you counsel with the Lord to see if medicine was for you?" I had to hang my head and reply, "Ah . . . um . . . ah . . . no, sir." "Then let this be a learning experience for you. You get on your knees and plead with the Lord to help you find your niche. He will." I'll always remember those words "your niche." I wondered why he picked them, but it reminded me of a story I heard President Hugh B. Brown tell in a conference in Sao Paulo, Brazil. The story, "I'm the Gardner Here," has since become a classic, and it gave me great comfort.

When Elder Brown was young he lived on a farm. On the farm grew a large, wild current bush. Being wild, the fruit was very sparse. So one day he took an axe and pruned down the current bush so it would send out new shoots that would be fruitful. As he stood back and watched the sap drip out of the stubbed branches, he imagined he heard the bush cry to him, "Why have you been so cruel? I was growing fine. I wanted to be as tall as that apple tree and I was almost there. Why did you cut me down?" He then answered out loud and said, "I'm sorry little bush, but I'm the gardner here. I know what's best for you and I did it for your own good. Someday you'll see, someday you'll give forth good fruit, but as a current bush, not an apple tree."

Some years later, he was in England in the army as a major. He was being considered for a high position, and because of his excellent record, the position was sure to be his. One night his commander called him into his office, and there he was told that another man had been given the position. As they were talking, the commander was called out of the office. There, laying open on the desk, were the records of Elder Brown. He leaned over the desk and took a look at them. There in large black letters were written the words, "This man is a Mormon." Elder Brown turned and left the room knowing why he had not received the position.

He passed back through the camp until he arrived at his tent and there he looked up into the starry night and clenched his fist and cried, "God, why have you been so cruel? I was progressing fine. Why have you cut me down?" Then, in the silence, the words he said to the current bush came back into his mind, "I'm sorry little bush, but I'm The Gardner here. I know what's best for you and I did it for your own good. Someday you'll see, someday you'll bring forth good fruit, but as a current bush, not an apple tree."[24]

What "good fruit" I was to bring forth I had absolutely no idea; but I now knew I wasn't to be an apple tree. During this time I reflected on two of life's important lessons I learned from this catastrophe: counsel with the Lord to find your niche, and once you find it, work hard and work smart. I had done neither.

So now I began to pray in earnest. For the next 2½ years I wore out my knees, tried one college major after another, interviewed with countless companies. Nothing seemed right. In the meantime I married, became a father, and started a small mail-order chemical business which I absolutely loved! I also reverted back to a hobby I had as a kid of making fireworks. I was coming up with new ideas and chemicals to sell to the fireworks trade, and making money at it! My answer from the Lord came indirectly and unexpectedly, as many do. At a party, a friend told me I should go back to Utah and start a fireworks factory. That was it! The answer was so simple, but it was like a light went on inside my head! I knew and felt that he was right. It rang true. The Spirit confirmed it. It was my answer from the Lord!

We did come back to Utah and start a fireworks factory. My wife and I both worked long, hard, dirty hours at it. We would sometimes put the kids to sleep in the back of our station wagon so we could work until 1 a.m. Then I'd be back at it at 8 a.m., but I loved it! Though my sweet wife didn't "love" it, she fully supported me. Many people thought I was crazy, but I kept at it. I could stay at it despite much adversity because this was my niche.

The Lord "gave me fire for the deed." Those who heard of my enterprise called it foolish. Some mocked me and laughed, but who can doubt that the Holy Ghost inspired me. The Lord with provident hand unlocked my mind, inspiring me with patentable ideas—whole new processes and formulas that had not been used in the trade before. As a result, our company became very successful in international competition because of our unique effects. I believe the Lord will do this for any of us as we find our niches and missions.

Before I was called as a mission president, I made my living at two things I love to do: making fireworks, and improvising piano music at a melodrama summer theater. As a teenager I wrote the Disney studio and asked how to get into the business of composing cartoon music. They didn't tell me, but melodrama music is definitely cartoon music! So if I can fill such insignificant professional niches as composing cartoon music and making fireworks, anyone can find and fill their niches too. As the title of a book says, *Do What You Love, the Money Will Follow*.

Writing your mission-vision does not make you immune from setbacks or detours. But if you've "taken the Holy Spirit to be your guide" and based your writing on gospel principles you'll return to your correct course. Said Elder Marvin J. Ashton, "The wind and waves will periodically interfere with our chosen course, even in financial matters; but the laws of the gospel can bring us back on course and guide us to peaceful waters."[25]

Interestingly, humans are the only creatures that can both laugh and cry. That's probably because we're the only ones that know the difference between what is and what ought to be. A mission-vision helps us to understand what ought to be.

You're here on earth to be happy, to have joy. This doesn't mean you won't have problems, disappointments, adversity, pain, and suffering. But by expending the energy to create a mission-vision, you'll be able to better survive your trials. At times, it may be the only way you can survive them.

One time we had an explosion that literally wiped out our fireworks plant. No one was hurt, but I went through some deep pain and soul searching, wondering if I should rebuild and if I even was in the right profession. After pleading with the Lord, I remembered my spiritual confirmation to what my professional niche was. We did rebuild, and our company became even more successful.

A mission-vision helps keep you from the energy draining, negative activity of second guessing yourself. A mission-vision helps you to survive setbacks and discouragement because, with your mission, you know these setbacks are only temporary. Knowing where you want to go gives a strong sense of wanting to get there, buoying you up with the confidence and energy to overcome doubt, fear and uncertainty and all the obstacles that are such an integral part of life. With a mission-vision you can be like Abraham, and other Biblical stalwarts of faith who "in faith, not having received the promises, but having seen them afar off, and were persuaded of them, embraced them" (Heb. 11:13).

John S. Tanner cited a profound truth when he observed,

> Uncertainty can be more chilling than winter, doubt more gnawing than hunger. Not knowing when or if an affliction will end is often more taxing than the affliction itself . . . I am reminded of the ending of The Pilgrim's Progress, which portrays Christian and Hopeful crossing the river of death. There "was no bridge to go over and the river was very deep." The two pilgrims begin to despair, for there is no way across except through. Then they learn this truth: "You shall find the river deeper or shallower, as you believe in the King of this place."[26]

Writing your mission-vision helps you "see the promises afar off and be persuaded by them," so you can eventually "embrace" them. It helps you overcome the fear, uncertainty and doubt of a "deeper" river, keeping it as shallow as possible.

Understand, if you don't have the energy to write your mission-vision, you probably won't have the energy to do anything else about it. You may think I'm belaboring the point of writing. It may seem unnecessary or too simple to make a difference. It is not. "Now ye may suppose that this is foolishness in me; but behold I say unto you, that by small and simple things are great things brought to pass; and small means in many instances doth confound the wise" (Al. 37:6). Galileo and Lincoln both thought that the most important invention was writing. It is one of those small and simple things by which great things are brought to pass.

A mission-vision will not make you immune from the anxiety and doubt of not being able to see your whole mission at once. Although it will help a lot, you will still have to be satisfied by saying to the Lord the words of the hymn *Lead, Kindly Light*:[27]

Lead, kindly Light, amid th' encircling gloom;
    Lead thou me on!
The night is dark, and I am far from home;
    Lead thou me on!
Keep thou my feet; I do not ask to see

The distant scene—one step enough for me.

Elder Boyd K. Packer taught this principle:

> I had been called as an Assistant to the Council of the Twelve, and we were to move to Salt Lake City and find an adequate and permanent home . . . A home was located that was ideally suited to our needs. Elder Harold B. Lee came and looked it over very carefully and then counseled, "By all means, you are to proceed."
>
> But there was no way we could proceed. I had just completed the course work on a doctor's degree and was writing the dissertation. With the support of my wife and our eight children, all our resources we could gather over the years had been spent on education. By borrowing on our insurance, gathering every resource, we could barely get into the house, without sufficient left to even make the first monthly payment. Brother Lee insisted, "Go ahead. I know it is right."
>
> I was in deep turmoil because I had been counseled to do something I had never done before—to sign a contract without having the resources to meet the payments. When Brother Lee sensed my feelings he sent me to President McKay, who listened carefully as I explained the circumstances. He said, "You do this. It is the right thing." But he extended no resources to make it possible.
>
> When I reported to Brother Lee he said, "That confirms what I have told you." I was still not at peace, and then came the lesson. Elder Lee said, "Do you know what is wrong with you—you always want to see the end from the beginning."
>
> I replied that I wanted to see at least a few steps ahead. He answered by quoting from Ether 12:6: "Wherefore, dispute not because ye see not, for ye receive no witness until after the trial of your faith."
>
> And then he said, "My boy, you must learn to walk to the edge of the light, and perhaps a few steps into the darkness, and you will find that the light will appear and move ahead of you." And so it had—but only as we walked to the edge of the light.
>
> We have not yet moved to the edge of the light, either as individuals or as a church. We have not used all of the resources yet available to us. I am confident that as we move to the edge of the light, like the cloud that led the Israelites, or like the star that led the wise men, the light will move ahead of us.[28]

A mission-vision helps you "see and use all the resources yet available to you" so you can then "walk to the edge of the light, and perhaps a few steps into the darkness."

You are the only one who can perform your mission. As Elder H. Burke Peterson said, "There are things for each of you to do that no one else can do as well as you."[29]

Each of us has strong points that the Lord can use. Remember, in Jacob's allegory of the tame and wild olive trees, he said that ". . . the servants did go forth and labor with their mights" (Jac. 5:72). Notice the plural "mights." "The Lord uses us because of our unique personalities and differences, rather than in spite of them. He needs all of us, with our blemishes and weaknesses and limitations," said Patricia T. Holland.[30]

A story told by Lisa Nock, adapted from George H. Reavis, illustrates this.

> Once upon a time, the animals decided to do something to meet the problems of the world. So, they organized a school with a curriculum of running, climbing, swimming, and flying. To make it easier to administer, all the animals took all the subjects.
>
> The duck was excellent in swimming. In fact, he was better than his instructor. But, he made only passing grades in flying; and he was really poor in running. Since he was slow in running, he had to stay after school to practice running, and he had to drop swimming. This caused his little web feet to be so badly worn that after that he was only average in swimming. But, average was quite acceptable, so no one worried about that—except for the duck.
>
> The rabbit started at the top of his class in running. But he developed a nervous twitch in his leg from so much make-up work in swimming. The squirrel was excellent in climbing. But he encountered constant frustration in flying class, because his teacher made him start from the ground up instead of from the tree-top down. He developed charlie horses from so much exertion, so he ended up with only a "C" in climbing, and a "D" in running. The eagle was a real problem child and he was severely disciplined for being a non-conformist. In climbing classes he beat all the others to the top of the tree. But he insisted in flying to get there.
>
> Now the moral of this story is that everybody has their own set of capabilities in which they will naturally succeed, unless they are expected or forced to fit a mold that they really don't fit. If you're a duck, don't try to be a great runner. You were meant to swim.[31]

A great article by Douglas Malloch emphasizes this message. It's entitled "Be the Best of Whatever You Are."

> We all dream of great deeds and high positions, away from the pettiness and humdrum of ordinary life. Yet success is not occupying a lofty place or doing conspicuous work; it is being the best that is in you. Rattling around in too big a job is worse than filling a small one to over-flowing. Dream, aspire by all means; but do not ruin the life you must lead by dreaming pipe dreams of the one you would like to lead. Make the most of what you have and are. Perhaps your trivial, immediate task is your one sure way of proving your mettle. Do the thing near at hand, and great things will come to your hand to be done.

If you can't be a pine on the top of the hill,
Be a scrub in the valley—but be
The best little scrub by the side of the rill;
Be a bush if you can't be a tree.
If you can't be a bush be a bit of grass,
And some highway happier make;
If you can't be a muskie then just be a bass —
But the liveliest bass in the lake!
We can't all be captains, we've got to be crew,
There's something for all of us here,
There's big work to do, and there's lesser to do,
And the task you must do is the near.
If you can't be a highway then be just a trail,
If you can't be the sun be a star;
It isn't by size that you win or you fail —
Be the best of whatever you are!

Emmett Miller, a noted psychiatrist, said this about living something other than your mission.

> Attempting to live up to the demands, expectations, goals and dreams of other people is indeed a quest for fool's gold. No matter how grand your accomplishment, if it does not reflect your own personal values, purpose and dreams, the victory will be hollow. You end up feeling like you are wearing somebody else's clothes—the fit isn't quite right, the colors are awful, and you just don't feel comfortable wearing them.[32]

Elder Groberg taught:

> Reaffirm in our lives the importance of at least three things: first, our Father in Heaven does have a specific mission for all of us to fulfill and perform while we are here upon this earth; second, that we can, here and now in this life, discover what that mission is; and third, that with His help we can fulfill that mission and know and have assurance—here and now in this life —that we are doing that which is pleasing to our Father in Heaven.[33]

Remember what happened in the film "The Lion King" when he forgot who he was? When he forgot he was the son of the king and had a great mission to complete, he fled from his responsibilities when adversity came. Some time later, with the help of the wise baboon, the spirit of his father said to him: "My son, you forgot *who you are* and thus forgot me. You are my son; you are the son of the king; you were born to be the king."

This recognition of his great mission gave him the strength to return and complete it. But note well: it was not until he recognized who he was—the son of the king—that he recognized that he had a great mission to do and was then able to muster the force to continue, to persevere, to achieve his potential—"the measure of his creation."

You, too, are the son or daughter of The King, and you were born to one day be a king or queen. To prepare you for this, The King has given you a great mission to complete. Going through the mission-vision process is a powerful experience that empowers you with spiritual energy to better detect and live your life's mission. Being the real you is really being true. Shakespeare was right on target when he said, "To thine own self be true."

Detect and live your life's mission and mini-missions to better

KEEP THE SPIRIT!

15

CHOOSE AND RECORD YOUR VALUES — WRITE YOUR OWN CONSTITUTION —

Nothing gives so much direction to a person's life as a sound set of principles.

—Ralph Waldo Emerson

The unexamined life is not worth living.

—Plato

Each of us is largely the product of his or her beliefs. Our behavior is governed by these. They become our standard of conduct.

—President Gordon B. Hinckley

Governing values are the attributes, virtues or character traits that give foundation to your life. They are important because what you value, you think about; and what you think about, you become. As the proverb says, "As [a man] thinketh in his heart, so is he" (Prov. 23:7). All your decisions are based on what you really value. The values to base your mortal life on are the same ones your spirit learned, lived, and cherished in your premortal existence. As you live these values, you remain true to your original self since you continue to "keep" your "first estate" while you live here on earth in your "second estate" (Abr. 3:22-26).

You need to use this second estate to increase your power over the properties of earth life (time, physical matter, and space). Satan would like to imprison you within these. Your governing values should increase your freedom. To have the opportunity to become as free as Father in Heaven is free is one of the reasons "the morning stars sang together, and all the sons of God shouted for joy" (Job 38:7).

Satan tries to deceive you into adopting the pseudo values of "the world" instead of maintaining the true values you learned and kept in your first estate. Paul warned, "Beware lest any man spoil you through philosophy and vain deceit, after the traditions of men, after the rudiments of the world, and not after Christ" (Col. 2:8). By adopting Satan's values, you develop a counterfeit identity in place of your original self. He would have you measure your worth by the "Four P's" of worldly wealth: possessions, performance, position, and 'ppearance. He would deceive you into believing that these things *are* yourself, your real self.

Satan would have you compare yourself with others, supposedly to see if you measure up. If you value yourself by comparisons, then there is always somebody that is better than you in any particular subject. If you choose to live by comparisons, you'll win some but lose a lot. The pressure is always on: there's always the pressure to say the right things, wear the right clothes, and make the right impressions. Recall all the scoffing that came from those in the "great and spacious building" in Lehi's dream (1 Nephi 8:26).

Ben Franklin observed that, "The eyes of other people are the eyes that ruin us. If all but myself were blind, I should want neither fine clothes, fine houses, nor fine furniture." If you compare yourself, you deny yourself your own uniqueness. When you live by comparisons and don't measure up, you feel terrible. Satan uses your sorrow, lack of self-esteem, and depression as his tool. When you compare yourself with others and appear in some way to be better than they, then pride becomes the issue and the turf Satan uses to tempt you. When you live by comparisons, you develop blame for yourself, for others, and for things "out there."

The values you should select are set forth in the scriptures and in your Patriarchal Blessing, your own personal scripture. The 13th Article of Faith lists some of these values. When you begin to diligently "seek after these things," you come to know and magnify the values you learned in your first estate. These traits will help you "subdue" the earth; develop loving, eternal relationships; and overcome Satan's influences. From another perspective, the values you need to pick are based on the ones that will enhance the three relationships given by the Savior in Matt. 22:37-40: your relationship with God, with yourself, and with others.

To draw these teachings out of the scriptures and into your life involves asking yourself the following or similar questions and listening, or rather feeling inwardly, what your heart is communicating to you: What do I value most in life? What matters most to me? What are my highest priorities? What character traits would I like to develop, base my life on, and have as a personal code of conduct? When my life is over, what will I be glad I did and became?

The answers to these questions form a firm foundation for discovering the values on which you should base your life's mission. Answering these questions is the way you "liken all scriptures unto us, that it might be for our profit and learning" (1 Ne. 19:23). This is the way you personalize the scriptures to yourself. You literally take spiritual truths—the values you lived in your first estate—into your own hands and begin to transfer them from the scriptures into your own character as you write them down and live them. As the hymn says, "Let each man learn to know himself; To gain that knowledge let him labor."[1]

Little by little, "line upon line, precept upon precept" your earthly values become congruent with the values you treasured in your pre-earth life. You gradually become more empowered to govern your life and your missions with these values instead of being governed by your moods. You cannot catch the vision of your mission in this earthly life unless you're standing on the same firm foundation of truth that you stood on in the pre-earth life.

You need to write these values down to show yourself and the Lord you have "real intent" to live by them. There may be several things you think you're committed to living that may not stand the test of real stress, or may give way to your rationalizations if you don't write them down. The physical activity of writing bridges the gap from merely thinking about something to physically doing it. The process of writing is what empowers you to do this.

As you liken the scriptures to yourself, you become more capable of actually performing the principle; and the doing is what changes your very inner self, your character. Writing is the process that makes the doing more likely to happen. By writing, you take the physical flesh and bone of a principle and give it a spirit—life—as you define it, so it means something to you.

Elder Russell M. Nelson of the Quorum of the Twelve taught this idea when discussing how to observe the Sabbath. He said, "I plead with you to do more than passively follow lists of do's and don'ts compiled by others. Generate your own policies, and live by them."[2]

Here's what Bishop J. Richard Clarke, quoting Robert Brenchley, had to say about the danger of non-commitment to values, or the even greater peril of having no values:

> One of my fears for the future stems from the fact that in recent years some of the nation's brightest, best educated, and most richly rewarded career people have committed acts that destroy careers and cancel all their bright promise. One interpretation is that they betrayed their values—for money, or power, or sensual pleasure. Another interpretation is that they didn't have any values to betray, that the values had been jettisoned long ago in the swift upward climb.[3]

If you are not willing to expend the minimal energy to write your values down in calm circumstances, chances are good that you won't have the energy to live them in an energy-draining crisis.

Here are some examples of what you could have on your list of values: self-worth, honesty, faith, family, service, humility, knowledge, chastity. Your list could contain 10 to 20 values. Ben Franklin's list had 13 "virtues," The Young Women's program has 7 values, The Scout Law has 12, President Hinckley lists 10.[4]

Once you've listed these, write a short paragraph for each one explaining what it means to you. Then prioritize these values by asking yourself these or similar questions: What do I value more than anything else in life? If I could only live three or four values, what would they be?

Writing down your values will be one of your most enjoyable projects—ever! You'll probably spread this exercise over several weeks as you ponder and digest the truths in the scriptures and then express these in your own words. In this way, you liken the scriptures unto yourself for your profit and learning.

Values help pull you, rather than push you, toward what you want to become or do. Pull implies you have the freedom to choose: to accept or reject, fulfill or forfeit, the benefits.

Charles Schurz said, "Ideals are like stars. You will not succeed in touching them with your hands; but, like the seafaring man, you choose them as your guides, and, following them, you reach your destiny."

Having a foundation of values based on eternal truths gives you one of the basic securities: knowing that you can cope, that you can make correct decisions. William Faulkner made this profound observation: "I have found that the greatest help in meeting any problem with decency and self-respect and whatever courage is demanded, is to know where you yourself stand. That is, to have in words what you believe and are acting from."

Living your values not only is necessary to "Catch the Vision of Your Mission," but it also helps you promote the Lord's work and to combat evil. Edmund Burke said, "The only thing necessary for the triumph of evil is for good men to do nothing."[5] If the "natural man" or "the flesh" were the only causes of evil, then evil would most likely not triumph among "good men." But Satan initiates evil, and his plan is served equally well by the lack of action of some as it is by the misdeeds of others.

A car in neutral can be as easily pushed backward as it can forward. A person in neutral—one who doesn't consciously try to do good—is by his inaction assisting Satan by default. The 13th Article of Faith clearly says "we *seek after* these things," not merely tolerate them. Remember the proverb, "If you don't stand for something, you'll fall for anything."

Satan does not now, and never has respected agency. Therefore, he takes the initiative to lead you away captive down to hell as he whispereth in your ear to do evil (2 Ne. 28:21-22). The Lord has always honored your agency. He will help you when you act on your own initiative; but He won't attempt to force you to do good, even though Satan forces evil.

Know this, that every soul is free
To choose his life and what he'll be;
For this eternal truth is giv'n:
That God will force no man to heav'n.

He'll call, persuade, direct aright,
And bless with wisdom, love, and light,
In nameless ways be good and kind,
But never force the human mind.[6]

Thus you can do good in only one way—by choosing to do so. But conversely, you can promote evil in two ways: by choice or by default. Default, or doing nothing, is in reality a choice—a choice in this instance to move in the direction of evil or failure.

An excellent example is Elder Robert L. Backman's story about test pilots. If anything goes wrong with the plane, the pilot will decide to either bail out or try to land. He *will* make that decision sooner or later, even if he doesn't want to, because "no decision plus time equals a decision."[7]

Here's a great summation by Benjamin Franklin on the importance of governing your life on a system of values based on "correct principles."

> We stand at the crossroads, each minute, each hour, each day, making choices. We choose the thoughts we allow ourselves to think, the passions we allow ourselves to feel, and the actions we allow ourselves to perform. Each choice is made in the context of whatever value system we've selected to govern our lives. In selecting the value system, we are, in a very real way, making the most important choices we will ever make. Those who believe there is one God who made all things and who governs the world by His Providence will make choices different from those who do not. Those who hold in reverence that Being who gave them life and worship Him through adoration, prayer and thanksgiving will make choices different from those who do not. Those who believe that mankind are all of a family and that the most acceptable service to God is doing good to man will make many choices different from those who do not. Those who believe in a future state in which all that is wrong here will be made right will make choices different from those who do not. Those who subscribe to the morals of Jesus Christ will make many choices different from those who do not. Since the foundation of all happiness is thinking rightly, and since correct action is dependent on correct opinion, we cannot be too careful in choosing the value system we allow to govern our thoughts and actions. And to know that God governs in the affairs of men, that He hears and answers prayers, and that He is a rewarder of them that diligently seek Him, is indeed, a powerful regulator of human conduct.[8]

So, get started! First, make your list of values (*example*: Family). Next, write each of your values as an action statement (*example*: I love my family). Now, prioritize your list. Last, write a short paragraph for each value clarifying what the value means to you.

Probably the best way to get better at living your values is to follow the example of Benjamin Franklin. He tried to live all of his values daily, but he emphasized and looked for ways to live a specific one each week. He would evaluate himself at the end of each day. A good way to do this is to have a simple form in your planner with the following information:

VALUE OF THE WEEK

____

Today's Date: ________________________________

What will I do to practice this value today? ________________

____

____

____

My score on how I kept this value today: (1 to 10) ____________

Good Points: ________________________________

____

____

Weak Points: ________________________________

____

____

What I will do to be better tomorrow: ____________________

____

____

As you fine-tune your values with the help of the Spirit, you will more and more embrace, live, and cherish the same values you lived in the pre-earth life. You will be better able to recognize and live your overall mission and your several mini-missions, and you will be better able to

KEEP THE SPIRIT!

16

AVOID SPIRITUAL CRUISE CONTROL

Make something of your lives. It isn't enough just to exist; make a contribution to society of which we are a part.
—President Gordon B. Hinckley[1]

As a returned missionary you are now a veteran of the "time trials" for the "Spiritual Indy 500." Here are some concluding reminders of some road hazards to keep you from going on "spiritual cruise control."

1. Up till now, your mission probably was the greatest spiritual experience of your life. But at your homecoming, I hope you won't merely say, "It was the best two years of my life!" I hope you'll add, "until now." The rest of your life can be even more satisfying than your mission if you look at its various activities and seasons in the same way you looked at your mission when you had the most gratifying times. You succeeded best—even excelled—when you had the perspective that what you did was a stewardship for the glory of God.

Your life, too, is a stewardship from God. You're here on earth to serve God's purposes. Earth life is not a stage on which to act out your own selfish desires and ambitions. If you look at all aspects of your life—dating, marriage, education, profession, family life, church service—as an ongoing stewardship or a mission from God, you can develop the correct attitudes to not only succeed, but to excel. When any aspect of your life becomes self-serving, it becomes spiritually unsatisfying. Remember, there's a big difference between "self-service" and "selfless service."

If you look upon each role in your life as the fulfilling of an ongoing mission for the glory of God, you will have even greater spiritual rewards and experiences than you did in the mission field. As Stephen Covey says, "you won't need to live on the sweet memories and resurrected testimony of your mission days as the source of your spiritual life."[2] You'll be creating "the best two years of your life" as you live each two years, if you **KEEP THE SPIRIT!**

2. Your primary purpose in the "real world," like the mission field, is to serve, not to be served. Thus, the Lord arranged your life experience so you are a steward of everything. This includes your agency, time, mortal body, talents, opportunities, wealth—everything! And you will give an accounting to the Lord of these stewardships. This is why your giving to the Lord your personal offering of "a broken heart and a contrite spirit" is so meaningful (3 Ne. 9:20). As you do this, you more fully can **KEEP THE SPIRIT!**

3. Many RM's told me they "weren't doing anything important" since they left the mission field. I'd reply they needed to repent about calling "not important" what the Lord assigned to Adam when he said, "By the sweat of thy face shalt thou eat bread" (Moses 4:25). "Real world" work is important; doing "real world" work is the only way you can learn many of the lessons you came to this earth to learn! Adam and Eve are our examples; we need to *work* out our salvation, as they did in the "real world."

You'll have many opportunities to bless others and make this world a little less "lone and dreary" if you understand you truly are doing important work by learning how to provide yourself, family, and others with the necessities of this life. You'll also have to learn how to "wait upon the Lord" as they did, something Satan never could learn. There are many things to learn in the "real world" that were impossible to learn in the mission field. Recognize and acknowledge that when you were released from your mission, it was merely a transfer to another area to learn and serve the Lord in an expanded way—a way in which you learn how to **KEEP THE SPIRIT!** in an expanded area—the "real world."

4. Work hardsmartuf, with inner discipline, but with paced excellence. Do this in both "real world" and spiritual endeavors. Said Elder James E. Talmage about the Parable of the Unjust Steward (Lk. 16:1-13): "Our Lord's purpose was to show the contrast between the care, thoughtfulness, and devotion of men engaged in the money-making affairs of earth, and the half-hearted ways of many who are professedly striving for eternal riches."[3] Doing the "Five Golden Rings" is the key which will turn you on to do the other things necessary to **KEEP THE SPIRIT!**

5. You cannot revert back to your old habits, nor "adapt" to the "real world" when you return. As an RM, you must now be an example to show others the way of how they, too, can **KEEP THE SPIRIT**! Here's why.

> A revealing conversation once occurred between the Prophet Joseph Smith and a brother named Isaac Behunnin. He had seen men involved in the quorums and in the high spiritual experiences of the kingdom who had subsequently become disaffected, and it was a mystery to him why they had then devoted their zeal and energy to attacking the Church. He said to the Prophet: "If I should leave this Church I would not do as those men have done. I would go to some remote place where Mormonism had never been heard of, settle down, and no one would ever learn that I knew anything about it." The Prophet immediately responded: "Brother Behunnin, you don't know what you would do. Before you joined this Church you stood on neutral ground. When the Gospel was preached, good and evil were set before you. You could choose either or neither. There were two opposite masters inviting you to serve them. When you joined this Church you enlisted to serve God. When you did that you left neutral ground, and you can never get back to it. Should you forsake The Master you enlisted to serve it will be by the instigation of the evil one, and you will follow his dictation and be his servant."[4]

None of us, including you, are immune from the "instigation(s) of the evil one." As a bishop, I saw RMs think they could stay on "neutral ground," put themselves on "spiritual cruse control," and ease up doing the things that kept the Spirit with them. As a result, I heard some sad stories. Remember what happened to the RMs who were "lukewarm" in Revelation 3:16? Even more serious, remember this from Mormon and then from the Lord:

> And thus we can plainly discern, that after a RM has been once enlightened by the Spirit of God, and has had great knowledge of things pertaining to righteousness, and then has fallen away into sin and transgression, he becomes more hardened, and thus his state becomes worse than though he had never known these things (Al. 24:30, mais ou menos).

> Verily I say, RMs should be anxiously engaged in a good cause, and do many things of their own free will, and bring to pass much righteousness. But the RM that doeth not anything until he is commanded,

and receiveth a commandment with doubtful heart, and keepeth it with slothfulness, the same is damned (D&C 58:27,29, mais ou menos).

6. Moroni thought the counsel from his father, Mormon, on how to distinguish between good and evil so important for RMs to know in the latter days that he used what limited space he had left on the plates to include it (Moroni 7:12-18, especially verses 13 and 16). You will want to use this counsel frequently when judging the value of music, movies, videos, books—anything.

After a session at the Mission President's Training Seminar in which I had played a musical number on the piano, Elder Scott came up to me and said: "President, I want you to make me a promise that you will use your music as much as possible on your mission." In accordance with this, my family and I presented many fireside programs in which we explained and demonstrated the effects music has on us. Members brought their investigating friends for an evening of music and a Gospel discussion. I used this scripture in these firesides.

After one such fireside in Sao Paulo, a young man came up to me and said, "President Degn, are you familiar with the music of Pink Floyd?" I replied that I knew of the group. He said, "Is their music bad? I really like it." I asked, "Do you remember that scripture in Moroni 7 we read tonight? You can answer this question yourself." So he answered, "Well, the music must be good because it makes me feel really good when I listen to it." I said, "Well, let's read the scripture again." We read together in verse 13, ". . . wherefore, every thing which inviteth and enticeth to *do good*, and to *love God*, and to *serve him*, is inspired of God." "Irmao," [brother], I said, "the scripture says that for music to be good, it needs to 'invite and entice' you to *do good* and *serve God*. Does Pink Floyd do this to you?" He grew pensive. I asked him to look deep inside himself, be totally sincere, and answer with his conscience. I could tell the Spirit was there and was starting to touch him. He finally answered, "The music makes me want to stay in my room. I guess I don't want to get out and do anything, just stay in my room." "Who does the music entice you to serve," I asked. "Myself," he replied. "By using this scripture, you, yourself, can judge the merits of any music, or anything, for that matter," I said. "It's not totally how music makes you *feel*, but what and who it influences you *do, serve and love* that is important. Very harmful substances can temporarily make us feel good, but in the long run they are extremely harmful. Take alcohol, tobacco, and drugs for instance. The same with music. Feeling is important, but *what it entices you do do, whom it entices you to love,* and *whom it leads you to serve* are more important in determining if music, or anything, is good." He thanked me, and was off.

A "down home" way of stating Moroni's counsel would be from veteran musician Pete Seager, winner of the best folk album in the 39th annual Grammy Awards, when he said in his acceptance speech, "the important thing in music is not is it *good* music, but what is it *good for*."[5] Would Satan use anything less than the best music—or anything— to snare you? What is it "good for?" Be perceptive. Be totally familiar with Moroni 7:12-18; sense what anything entices you to do, serve, or love. "Are ye ashamed to take upon you the name of Christ?" (Morm. 8:38). Have the courage to make some changes in your music, entertainment—anything—if necessary, so you can better **KEEP THE SPIRIT**!

7. As an RM, you are a prize catch for Satan. He has declared war against you. He'll try the same tactics and sucker punches that you perhaps fell for before your mission, plus a lot of new ones. Let me quote from a letter I received from one of our strongest missionaries when he returned home.

> President, I want you to tell all of the returning missionaries just how eager Satan is to get us upon our return! I can see how easy it would be for an RM to fall after his service if he wasn't warned that Satan is going to work to rip him apart.
>
> I was home one week and I was thrown into the most dangerous situation I've ever been in. In my last interview you told me that Satan would use the same tricks he used before my mission to get us after the mission because they were successful once. Well, get yourself a bowl of popcorn and check this one out.
>
> I received a call from [a former girl friend] saying she was in town to visit her family and she wanted to see me. I told her to come over, made sure my parents were going to be here, and everything went great. She left, but a couple of days later she gave me a call before flying back, telling me she had some questions about the church and explained she was at a cousin's house.
>
> I cruised up to see her, but no cousin. That's when I started feeling uncomfortable. She told me her husband was in Japan. I felt even more uncomfortable. Then she started telling me how she still had feelings for me, threw her arms around me and sobbed. At this point I think I was close to cardiac arrest. I had to quickly push her away.

> I said I needed to go, and while leaving I told her that those feelings she had for me should be dead because she wasn't being fair to her husband.
>
> I walked briskly back to my truck and had difficulty driving as I thought back to what could have happened. I cannot believe this happened! I never thought I'd be placed in a situation so scary! This was a big testimony booster for me, however, because the Spirit totally told me what to do. It was as if he placed into my head the right words to say and into my body the courage to push her off and run.
>
> This situation helped out my Provident Promise list also. As soon as I got home I wrote Provident Promise number 1: "I will not put myself into situations that will tempt me to lower my standards or compromise who I am."
>
> The evil one is truly out to get us. Tell the returning missionaries that it is dangerous out here and if we don't have the Spirit he's gonna nail us.[6]

I love the symbol of the Holy Ghost as a dove. Whether or not you keep the Spirit alive in you, or you crush the Holy Ghost's influence by choice—or neglect—is in your hands.

> In an ancient Greek village lived a famous wise man who could always answer on the spot any question put to him. One day, a young man told a friend: "I know how I can fool this wise man. I'll put a bird in my hand and ask the wise man if the bird is dead or alive. If he says it is alive, I'll squeeze the bird and kill it and let it fall to the ground; but if he says it is dead, I'll open my hand and let it fly away. Thus, the youth went to the wise man and asked: "O wise man, is the bird in my hand dead or alive?" The wise man looked at the young man and said: "My boy, the answer is in your hands."

As an RM, the answer to whether you keep the Holy Spirit with you or not is just as literally in your hands. As an RM, not only can you keep the Spirit with you to be safe and succeed, but you can excel in the "real world."

8. One of the most important reasons for wanting to **KEEP THE SPIRIT!** is to have access to personal revelation at this critical time of our life. You've had lots of experience in receiving it, but even with this experience, it sometimes is difficult to recognize the delicate promptings, especially if you've clouded your receptors with irreverent sights and sounds.

King Benjamin sounded as if he were addressing a gathering of RMs about this subject:

> And now, I say unto you [put your name here], my brethren, that after ye have known and have been taught all these things, if ye should transgress and go contrary to that which has been spoken, that ye do withdraw yourselves from the Spirit of the Lord, that it may have no place in you to guide you in wisdom's paths that ye may be blessed, prospered, and preserved . . . (Mosiah 2:36).

Elder Packer taught us about the danger of irreverent "entertainment:"

> This trend to more noise, more excitement, more contention, less restraint, less dignity, less formality is not coincidental nor innocent nor harmless.
>
> The first order issued by a commander mounting a military invasion is the jamming of the channels of communication of those he intends to conquer.
>
> Irreverence suits the purposes of the adversary by obstructing the delicate channels of revelation in both mind and spirit.[7]

I cannot stress this enough. I've seen too many RMs, innocently at first, involve themselves with inappropriate entertainment that wiped out their ability to **KEEP THE SPIRIT**! and receive personal revelation. This is so pervasive a danger and so crucial to an RM's spiritual health and temporal success, that I want to quote expansively from Elder H. Burke Peterson's last address as a General Authority. Elder Peterson believes that part of what Moroni had in mind in his last words of warning to us, "touch not the evil gift, nor the unclean thing" (Moroni 10:30), referred to some of today's music, videos and entertainment:

> My thoughts will center on our sometimes innocent involvement in one of the terrible, unclean things referred to by this ancient prophet. Satan, the very devil and father of all lies, has slyly and slowly lowered the social norms of morality to a tragic and destructive level. In magazines and books, on CDs and tapes, on our television and theater screens is portrayed more and more often a lifestyle that might even rival the excesses of those who lived in Sodom and Gomorrah. The screens, music, and printed materials, etc., are filled with a profusion of sex, nudity, and vulgarity.
>
> One of the great tragedies is that too many men and boys who hold the priesthood of God are watching and listening to this type of so-called entertainment. Some do it only casually at first. They think

they are spiritually strong and will be immune to its influence. This trash is nothing more nor less than pornography dressed in one of its many imitation robes of splendor—one of the master counterfeiter's best products.

Part of the tragedy I speak of is that many men and boys do not recognize they are trapped or soon will be. Unfortunately, I fear even some within the sound of my voice have an addiction and do not realize it. They see this as a form of entertainment that serves as a relief from the troubles of the day. In point of fact and reality, *it is only relieving them of their spirituality* and their capacity to draw on the powers of heaven in times of need . . . .

Brethren, I plead with you to leave it alone. Stay away from any movie, video, publication, or music—*regardless of its rating*—where illicit behavior and expressions are a part of the action. Have the courage to turn it off in your living room. Throw the tapes and the publications in the garbage can, for that is where we keep garbage.

. . . It is my understanding that any time we look at or listen to the kind of material we have been speaking of—even in its mildest form—the light inside of us grows dimmer because the darkness inside increases. The effect of this is that we cannot think as clearly on life's challenges—be they business, church, social, family, or personal—because the channel to the source of all light for the solving of problems is cluttered with various unclean images. Our entitlement to personal revelation on any subject is severely restricted. We don't do as well in school or work. We are left more on our own, and as a result we make more mistakes and we are not as happy. Remember, our mind is a wonderful instrument. It will record and keep whatever we put into it, both trash and beauty. When we see or hear anything filthy or vulgar, whatever the source, our mind records it, and as it makes the filthy record, beauty and clean thoughts are pushed into the background. Hope and faith in Christ begin to fade, and more and more, turmoil and discouragement are our companions.

Again I say, leave it alone. Turn it off, walk away from it, burn it. Erase it, destroy it. I know it is hard counsel we give when we say movies that are R-rated, and many with PG-12 ratings, are produced by satanic influences. Our standards should not be dictated by the rating system. I repeat, because of what they *really* represent, these types of movies, music, tapes, etc, serve the purposes of the author of all darkness.

Brethren, let's consider again why we cannot be involved in Satan's program of entertainment and be held guiltless. Why? because *we are men and boys of the covenant*, and that makes us different from all others. When we've made a covenant with the Lord, we are special—not ordinary, but special. He loves all of his sons, *but those of the covenant have a special responsibility.*[8]

9. We all need to understand, and especially RMs, that Satan is in all-out warfare against the Lord, His Church, the saints—and you. It is a continuation of the war we fought in the pre-mortal existence. I believe this is one of the main reasons why Mormon was inspired to include 21 chapters at the end of the book of Alma on warfare (Alma, chapters 43-63). He even includes many small details as to the prosecution of battles and warfare in general. He wanted us to be prepared for fighting a war—a spiritual war—but this time fought in a physical body.

A friend told me about a fireside he attended in Salt Lake City at the home of the patriarch of his stake some years ago. The patriarch was speaking about the importance of the youth knowing who they really were. My friend, who was sitting in the back by the door, almost dropped off his chair when about half way through the meeting, the door gently opened and President David O. McKay quietly entered. You can imagine the effect this had on those in the room, but especially on the speaker! The Prophet told him to continue. The patriarch reminded them about the great responsibility the youth had in the latter days. He mentioned that they were continuing the same battle here they had fought in the premortal existence. He said that each of them was a captain in the Lord's army those eons ago.

After the talk, as the prophet was shaking hands with everyone, the patriarch asked him if he had been correct in saying that each of the youth was a captain in the Lord's army. He hoped that he hadn't exaggerated. President McKay said that the talk was wonderful, but that he was incorrect on that point, but not by exaggeration. He then said to the youth that they were not captains in the Lord's army in that great pre-mortal war, but that each one had been a general. He then admonished them to remember who they were and fight accordingly because the battle is still raging.[9]

The following is good advice from Elder H. Burke Peterson:

Once in a while we should stop and ask ourselves, "In whose army are we fighting? Whose battle lines are we defending?" Do you have the courage to walk out of an off-color PG-rated move—or do you watch and listen and suggest to yourself, "This soon will pass"

> or "Everyone is doing it, it must be an acceptable type of entertainment." Have you the courage to keep out of your home some television shows that are filled with suggestive sexual conversation—and even some experiences? Have you thought lately how effective these shows are in piercing even the strongest spirits? Brethren, we must not feed ourselves a diet of trash![10]

LeGrand Richards taught that Satan wanted to destroy Moses and the Savior when they were babes and Joseph Smith when he was a young man. He knew that if he didn't do it then while they were young, he would have to reckon with Moses and Joseph Smith as prophets and with the Savior as the Messiah.[11] So it is with you. If Satan cannot destroy you now as an RM by poisoning you with a "diet of trash" or any other way, he will have to deal with you later as a more powerful father, or mother, and leader. You were a general in the Lord's pre-mortal forces, one of the "noble and great ones" (Abr. 3:22), you are so now. As I handed their release certificate to our missionaries, I'd say that it was also a graduation diploma for completing a Ph.D. in Life Preparation from the Lord's "East Point Academy" and a re-commission as a general in His earthly army. As a general, it is now your glorious responsibility to continue your training, to continue to **KEEP THE SPIRIT!** and to become a "leading man [or woman] who has influence, one who is in high places who can persuade others not to become servants of Satan."[12]

With all my love, I counsel you to do the same things that brought you success in the mission field—throughout your life, do the things that help you magnify your mission and

KEEP THE SPIRIT!

Endnotes

Introduction

1. Covey, Stephen R. 1971. *Spiritual Roots of Human Relations*. Salt Lake City: Deseret Book, p. 336.

Chapter 2

1. Tanner, John S. 1992. "One Step Enough." *BYU Speeches of the Year (1991-1992)*, p. 118.

Chapter 3

1. Medved, Michael. 1994. "Popular Culture and the War Against Standards." *This People*, Spring, p. 21.
2. *Church News*. September 2, 1995, p. 16.
3. *Journal of Discourses*. Volume 6, p. 98.

Chapter 4

1. Kimball, Spencer W. 1969. *The Miracle of Forgiveness*. Salt Lake City: Bookcraft pp. 284-286.
2. *The Herald Journal*, 13 Jan 1992, p. 17
3. Ballam, Michael. n.d. *Developing Divine Power* videotape. Logan: Phoenix Productions.
4. *Ibid.*
5. Richards, LeGrand. 1981. "Call of the Prophets." *Ensign*, May, p. 32.
6. Backman, Milton V., Jr. 1980. *Joseph Smith's First Vision*. Salt Lake City: Bookcraft, p. 174.
7. Kimball, Spencer W. 1982. *Teachings of Spencer W. Kimball*. Salt Lake City: Bookcraft, p. 301.
8. McGinnis, Alan. 1990. *The Power of Optimism*. San Francisco: Harper & Row, p. 66.
9. Clarke, J. Richard. "Choice—The Crucible of Character," *BYU Speeches of the Year (1988-1989)*, p. 99.

Chapter 5

1. Kimball, Spencer W. 1981. *Faith Precedes the Miracle.* Salt Lake City: Deseret Book, p. 110.
2. Madsen, Truman, 1989. *Joseph Smith the Prophet.* Salt Lake City: Bookcraft, p. 88.
3. Ashton, Marvin J. 1979. "Roadblocks to Progress." *Ensign.* May, p. 68.
4. Kimball, Spencer W. 1981. *Faith Precedes the Miracle.* Salt Lake City: Deseret Book, p. 195.
5. Lundwall, N.B. nd. *A Compilation Containing the Lectures on Faith.* Salt Lake City: Bookcraft, p. 71.
6. *Come Unto Jesus*, LDS Hymnal, Hymn 117.

Chapter 6

1. Benson, Ezra Taft. 1988. *Teachings of Ezra Taft Benson.* Salt Lake City: Bookcraft, p. 32.
2. Weldon, Joel. 1983, *Build a Better You* audio tapes. Chicago: Nightingale-Conant Corporation.
3. Ballam, Michael. *op. cit.*
4. Harmetz, Aljean. 1996. *On the Road to Tara: the Making of Gone with the Wind.* New York: Harry N. Abrams, Inc. pp. 68-69.
5. Covey, Stephen R. 1971. *The Spiritual Roots of Human Relations.* Salt Lake City: Deseret Book, p. 323.

Chapter 7

1. Benson, Ezra Taft. 1988. "The Law of Chastity." *BYU Speeches of the Year (1987-1988)*, p. 51.
2. Kimball, Spencer W. 1981. *Faith Precedes the Miracle.* Salt Lake City: Deseret Book, p. 177.
3. Cook, Gene R. 1991. *13 Lines of Defense.* Salt Lake City: Deseret Book, audiocassette.
4. Harrison, Grant Von. 1986. *Is Kissing Sinful?* Woods Cross: Publishers Books Sales, p. 7.
5. Tanner, N. Eldon. 1974. "No Greater Honor: The Woman's Role." *Ensign*, January, pp. 7-8.
6. Wright, Randal A. 1993. *Why Do Good People See Bad Movies?* National Family Institute. pp. 81-82.
7. Cook. *op. cit.*
8. Maxwell, Neal A. 1993. "Behold, the Enemy Is Combined." *Ensign*, May, p. 76.
9. Benson, Ezra Taft. 1986. "To the Youth of the Noble Birthright." *Ensign*, May, p. 45.

10. Holland, Jeffery R. 1988. "Of Souls, Symbols, and Sacraments." *BYU Speeches of the Year (1987-1988)*, pp. 73-75.
11. Hafen, Bruce C. 1983. "The Gospel and Romantic Love." *BYU Speeches of the Year (1982-1983)*, pp. 28-34.

Chapter 8

1. Ogden, D. Kelly. 1994. "The Sabbath Day." *Ensign*, April, p. 46.
2. "Cast Thy Burden upon the Lord," *Hymns*. 1985. The Church of Jesus Christ of Latter-day Saints. No. 110.
3. Faust, James E. 1991. "The Lord's Day." *Ensign*, November, 1991, p. 34.
4. Ogden. *Op. cit.*, pp. 49-50.
5. *Hymns*. No. 110.
6. No author. 1994. "Never on Sunday." *This People*, Spring, p. 11.
7. Didier, Charles. 1994. "Holy Day or Holiday?" *Ensign*, October, p. 30.
8. Covey, Stephen R. 1971. *Spiritual Roots of Human Relations*. Salt Lake City: Deseret Book, pp. 324-335.

Chapter 9

1. Benson, Ezra Taft. 1985. "What I Hope You Will Teach Your Children About the Temple." *Ensign*, August, p. 8.
2. Packer, Boyd K. 1990. "The Library of the Lord." *Ensign*, May, p. 38. (Elder Packer's emphasis.)
3. Kimball, Spencer W. 1982. *Teachings of Spencer W. Kimball*. Salt Lake City: Bookcraft, p. 390.
4. Benson, Ezra Taft. 1988. *Teachings of Ezra Taft Benson*. Salt Lake City: Bookcraft, p. 315.

Chapter 10

1. Levine, Daniel R.. "My First Job." *Reader's Digest*, January, 1996, p. 71.
2. Faust, James E. 1995. "Serving the Lord and Resisting the Devil." *Ensign*, September, p. 7.
3. Personal correspondence with the author. Used with permission.

Chapter 11

1. Perry, L. Tom. 1993. "Choose the Right." *Ensign*, November, p. 68.
2. Author unknown.
3. Benson, Ezra Taft. 1988. *A Witness and a Warning*. Salt Lake City: Desert Book, p. 8.
4. President Tanner also expressed this in writing in: *Prayer*. 1977. Salt Lake City: Deseret Book, p. 2.
5. Eyre, Linda, and Richard Eyre. 1982. *Teaching Children Responsibility*. Salt Lake City: Desert Book, p. 135.
6. Weldon, Joel. 1983. *Build a Better You* audio tapes. Chicago: Nightingale-Conant Corporation.

Chapter 12

1. *Missionary Handbook*. 1986. Salt Lake City: The Church of Jesus Christ of Latter-day Saints, p. 1.
2. Personal correspondence with the author. Used with permission. Emphasis his.
3. Tracy, Brian. 1984. *The Psychology of Achievement* audio tapes. Chicago: Nightingale-Conant Corporation.
4. Talmage, James E. 1960. *Jesus the Christ*. Salt Lake City: Deseret Book, p. 364.
5. McConkie, Bruce R. 1979. *Doctrinal New Testament Commentary*. Salt Lake City: Bookcraft, vol. 1, p. 515.

Chapter 13

1. McConkie, Bruce R. 1979. *Doctrinal New Testament Commentary*, Salt Lake City: Bookcraft, Vol. 1, p. 684.
2. Bureau of Land Management. 1990. *Hiking the Paria*, p. 2. Their emphasis.
3. Kimball, Spencer W. 1981. *President Kimball Speaks Out*. Salt Lake City: Deseret Book, p. 94.
4. Covey, Stephen R. 1971. *Spiritual Roots of Human Relations*. Salt Lake City: Deseret Book, pp. 326, 328.

Chapter 14

1. Yorgason, Blaine M. 1976. *Charlie's Monument*. Salt Lake City: Bookcraft. Used by permission.
2. Hinckley, Gordon B. 1993. "The Thing of Most Worth." *Ensign*, September, p. 2.
3. Cannon, George Q. 1957. *Gospel Truth*. Salt Lake City: Zion's Book Store, vol. 1, p. 22.

4. Peterson, H. Burke. 1979. "Your Special Purpose Here." *New Era*, May, pp. 4-5.
5. Frankl, Viktor E. 1963. *Man's Search for Meaning*. New York: Pocket Books, a division of Simon & Schuster, p. 172.
6. *Ibid.* p. 157.
7. "I Will Follow God's Plan,"*Children's Song Book*. 1989. The Church of Jesus Christ of Latter-day Saints, p. 164.
8. *The New Dictionary of Thoughts*. 1961. Ralph Emerson Browns, ed. (no city), p. 584.
9. Kimball, Spencer W. 1982. *Teachings of Spencer W. Kimball*. Salt Lake City: Bookcraft, p. 316.
10. Hyde, Orson. *Journal of Discourses*. vol. 7, pp. 315-316.
11. Benson, Ezra Taft. 1979. "In His Steps." *BYU Speeches of the Year (1979)*, pp. 46-47.
12. Covey, Stephen R. 1989. *The 7 Habits of Highly Effective People*. New York: Simon & Schuster.
13. Covey, Stephen R. 1994. *First Things First*. New York: Simon & Schuster.
14. Covey, Stephen R. 1989. *The 7 Habits of Highly Effective People*, p. 105.
15. Emerson, Ralph Waldo. *The Oxford Dictionary of Quotations*. 1978. Oxford University Press, (no city). p. 201.
16. "Let Each Man Learn to Know Himself," *Hymns*, 1948, No. 91.
17. Weldon, Joel. 1983. *Build a Better You* audio tapes. Chicago: Nightingale-Conant Corporation.
18. Petersen, Mark E. 1975. *The Great Prologue*. Salt Lake City: Deseret Book, p. 25.
19. Benson, Ezra Taft. 1979. "In His Steps." *BYU Speeches of the Year (1979)*, p. 64.
20. Roosevelt, Theodore. 1992. *Bartlett's Familiar Quotations*, 16th ed., Justin Kaplan, ed., Little, Brown and Co., Boston, p. 565.
21. Smith, Emmett R. 1983. *Dream the Impossible* audiotape. Salt Lake City: Covenant Recordings.
22. Lee, Janet G. 1992. "Knowing When to Persevere and When to Change Direction." *BYU Speeches of the Year (1991-1992)*, p. 47.
23. Groberg, John H. 1979. "What Is Your Mission?" *BYU Speeches of the Year (1979)*, p. 92.
24. Although I heard President Brown tell this story live, there are several sources. Probably the most available is: *Memoirs*

of Hugh B. Brown: An Abundant Life. Edwin B. Firmage, editor. Salt Lake City: Signature Books, 1988, pp. 56-57.
25. Ashton, Marvin J. 1992. *One for the Money*. Salt Lake City: The Church of Jesus Christ of Latter-day Saints, p. 1.
26. Tanner, John S. 1992. "One Step Enough for Me." *BYU Speeches of the Year (1991-1992)*, p. 123.
27. "Lead, Kindly Light," *Hymns*. 1985. No. 97.
28. Packer, Boyd K. 1980. *The Holy Temple*. Salt Lake City: Bookcraft, pp. 184-185.
29. Peterson, H. Burke. 1979. "Your Special Purpose Here." *New Era*, May, p. 5.
30. Holland, Patricia T. 1989. "Filling the Measure of Your Creation." *BYU Speeches of the Year (1988-1989)*, p. 73.
31. Nock, Lisa. 1982. *Teens to the Top* audio tape. Chicago: Nightingale-Conant Corporation.
32. Miller, Emmett. 1987. *Power Vision* audio tape. Chicago: Nightingale-Conant Corporation.
33. Groberg, John H. 1979. "What Is Your Mission?" *BYU Speeches of the Year (1979)*, p. 92.

Chapter 15

1. "Let Each Man Learn to Know Himself," *Hymns*. 1948. The Church of Jesus Christ of Latter-day Saints. No. 91.
2. Nelson, Russell M. 1991. "Standards of the Lord's Standard-bearers." *Ensign*, August, 10.
3. Clarke, J. Richard. 1989. "Choice—The Crucible of Character." *BYU Speeches of the Year (1988-1989)*, p.100.
4. Hinckley, Gordon B. 1992. "I Believe." *Ensign*, August, p. 4.
5. Cited in Benson, Ezra Taft. *Teachings of Ezra Taft Benson*. Salt Lake City: Bookcraft, pp. 676-677.
6. "Know This That Every Soul Is Free," *Hymns*. 1985. The Church of Jesus Christ of Latter-day Saints. No. 240.
7. Backman, Robert L. 1983. *Take Charge of Your Life*. Salt Lake City: Deseret, p. 83.
8. Rogers, George L., editor. 1986. *Benjamin Franklin's The Art of Virtue: His Formula for Successful Living*. Eden Prairie, MN: Acorn Publishing, pp. 89-90.

Chapter 16

1. Hinckley, Gordon B. 1996. "Make Something of Your Lives." *Ensign*, September, p. 77.
2. Covey, Stephen R. 1971. *The Spiritual Roots of Human Relations*. Salt Lake City: Deseret Book, p. 336.

3. Talmage, James E. 1960. *Jesus the Christ*. Salt Lake City: Deseret Book, p. 364.
4. Madsen, Truman. 1978. *Joseph Smith the Prophet*. Salt Lake City: Bookcraft, pp. 52-53.
5. National Public Radio. 1997. "39th Grammy Awards Presented," Morning Edition, 27 February.
6. Personal correspondence with the author. Used with permission.
7. Packer, Boyd K. 1991. "Reverence Invites Revelation," *Ensign*, November, p. 22.
8. Peterson, H. Burke. 1993. "Touch Not the Evil Gift, Nor the Unclean Thing." *Ensign*, November, pp. 42-43. Emphasis in the original.
9. Personal conversation with the participant.
10. Peterson, H. Burke. 1980. "Purify Our Minds and Spirits." *Ensign*, November, p. 38.
11. Richards, LeGrand. 1981. "Call of the Prophets." *Ensign*, May, p. 32.
12. Kimball, Spencer W. 1969. *The Miracle of Forgiveness*. Salt Lake City: Bookcraft, p. 175.

INDEX

F

G

H

J

K

L

Q

R

S

About the Author

Ralph Degn graduated from the University of Utah with a Bachelor's degree in History and minors in English, Music, Chemistry and Zoology. After considering a career as a concert pianist, and attending George Washington Medical School for a year, he earned an M.A. from Georgetown University with the intent of going into international business. He soon realized, however, that what he really loved doing as a hobby could become a profession for him. He founded Fireworks West International, which he owned and operated for 21 years. During that time he developed new formulas and processes in the trade to make the industry safer. He was able to patent his ideas, write a book on fireworks, and see his company grow from a single room to become the largest manufacturer of exhibition fireworks in the U.S. His fireworks have been enjoyed in Disneyland, the Olympics, the Calgary Stampede, and in the Stockholm Water Festival in Sweden.

Ralph is an excellent pianist and has enjoyed playing the last 17 years for the Pickleville Playhouse at Utah's Bear Lake. He also enjoys giving community musical programs and firesides. Music has been a very important part of his life. For years he has given musical programs and magic shows to school children.

Ralph has a vital interest in young people. He has been heavily involved in Scouting, beginning with his calling as a Varsity Scout Leader in a ward where Scouting was virtually nonexistent. He challenged the 19 young men in his program to become Eagle Scouts and two years later, conducted an Eagle Court of Honor for all 19 of them, including three of his own sons. As Varsity Scout coach, he challenged the 19 young men in his charge that if over the next year and a half they all earned their Eagle rank and earned all the money necessary, they would go on a super activity to Hawaii. All flew there as Eagles.

Among his other callings in the Church, Ralph has served in Bishoprics of three different student wards at Utah State University. While counseling young people there as their Bishop, he realized that many of them were struggling to keep the same Spirit in their lives that they had enjoyed on their missions. It was during this time that Ralph formulated the ideas for this book, recognizing the need for the youth to have some guidance in this area.

While serving as Bishop, Ralph was called to preside over the Brazil Sao Paulo North Mission. He and his wife, Mary Ann, accompanied by three of their children, resided in Brazil from 1993-1996. With the encouragement of his Area Presidency, Ralph translated his manuscript into Portuguese, giving copies of it to each of his departing missionaries. The response from them has been overwhelming as they have expressed appreciation for the guidance it has given them.

The theme for his missionaries in Brazil was to “Work Miracles!”, and Ralph realized that if missionaries, or anyone else for that matter, were to work miracles in their own lives they would need to follow the principles presented in this book.

Ralph and Mary Ann are the parents of seven children and a foster Indian son. Five of their children are returned missionaries. The Degn family resides in River Heights, Utah.